SOCIAL POLICY RESEARCH UNIT

The Costs of Informal Care:

LOOKING INSIDE THE HOUSEHOLD

Caroline Glendinning

London: HMSO

ISBN 0 11 701660 8

This Discussion Paper is based on work funded by DHSS (now the Department
of Health and the Department of Social Security) but the opinions expressed are
those of the researcher alone.

SPRU Editorial Group
Sally Baldwin
Lorna Foster
Gillian Parker
Roy Sainsbury
Patricia Thornton

Editor for this paper: Gillian Parker

Acknowledgements

I would like to thank the following people for their help in carrying out the research on which this discussion paper is based:

for the pre-pilot interviews, the staff of Age Concern York and the Disabled in York Information and Advisory Service;

for the pilot interviews, Advisory and Development staff and field social work staff, North Yorkshire Social Services Department;

for the main interviews, Jean Martin and Nicola Robus at OPCS; staff in Airedale District Hospital, Bradford Social Services Department, Airedale Community Nursing Service and North Yorkshire Social Services Department;

colleagues in SPRU, especially Sally Baldwin and Dot Lawton, Sue Medd and Lorna Foster;

Jean Ashton, for her meticulous word processing;

last – but far from least – Janet Bower, for her sensitive, patient and conscientious interviewing.

The project was undertaken at the Social Policy Research Unit, University of York.

Caroline Glendinning
University of Manchester

Contents

Informal care: a growing concern

The demographic context

During the last decade, there has been growing concern about the increasing numbers of disabled and elderly people who are likely to need some degree of physical or social care. Between 1961 and 1981 the total population of elderly people increased by nearly one-third. During the current 20 year period, from 1981 to 2001, that overall increase is expected to slow down considerably; but the proportion of very elderly people (and hence those most likely to need some form of assistance and care) is expected to more than double (Henwood, 1990).

Concern about the growing numbers of frail elderly and disabled people likely to need help and care has been mirrored by an increasing awareness of those who are already involved in care-giving, on an informal basis, to relatives, neighbours and friends. In part, this awareness can be attributed to the growth of articulate organisations representing carers themselves. The Association of Carers was founded in 1981 and made a major contribution to raising the public profile of carers, a role which has been taken over and maintained since 1988 by the Carers National Association.

Recent research has also yielded detailed information on both the extensiveness and intensiveness of informal care-giving. The 1985 General Household Survey (GHS) estimated that 14 per cent of people aged 16 and over (some 6 million adults in total) were looking after or providing regular help to a sick, elderly or handicapped person. Of these, 1.4 million were spending at least 20 hours a week providing help or supervision and 3.7 million bore the main responsibility for providing care (Green, 1988). Estimates derived from the OPCS disability survey, using slightly different questions and definitions, suggest that there are 1.3 million main carers of adults and children disabled enough to need help with self-care and domestic tasks (Parker, 1990). These surveys, and the increasing articulateness of carers themselves, mean that the impact and consequences of 'community care' policies on those who actually provide the bulk of care are less likely to remain invisible than in the past.

Carers and 'community care' policies

Over the past decade, informal carers have figured with growing prominence in the development of policies of community care. Concern about the potential public expenditure implications of the growing numbers of elderly people has been related to assertions that the informal ('community', 'neighbourhood' or 'family') sector must play an increasingly important part in providing support and care. For example, the 1981 White Paper on services for the elderly stated that:

> . . . the primary sources of support and care for elderly people are informal and voluntary. These spring from the personal ties of kinship, friendship and neighbourhood . . . It is the role of public authorities to sustain and, where necessary, develop – but never to displace – such support and care. (DHSS, 1981, para. 1.9)

Sir Roy Griffiths' report on community care similarly took pains to point out that the bulk of the care needed by people with longstanding illness or disability is given by 'families, friends, neighbours and other local people' who are 'uniquely well placed to identify and respond to' the care needs of their relatives and friends. Indeed, affirmed Sir Roy, 'this is as it should be' (Griffiths, 1988, p. 5). These sentiments were reiterated in the Government's own subsequent proposals for the reorganisation of 'community care' funding and service provision:

> . . . the great bulk of community care is provided by friends, family and neighbours . . . many people make that choice and it is right that they should be able to play their part in looking after those close to them. (DH et al, 1989, p. 4)

As informal carers have, with increasing explicitness, been acknowledged as integral and indispensable elements in the delivery of community care, so their needs for support and help have also begun to be recognised. There is a considerable contrast between the quasi-community development approach to 'sustaining . . . networks' implied in the policy statements of the early 1980s and the explicitly interventionist stance of seeking out, identifying and responding to carers' needs, of more recent documents:

> . . . a key responsibility of statutory service providers should be to *do all they can* to assist and support carers . . . Help may take the form of providing advice and support as well as practical services such as day, domiciliary and respite care. (DH et al, 1989, p. 9; author's emphasis)

At the same time, these policies have not been without some fierce critics. A steady stream of feminist research has highlighted the particularly heavy burdens of care-giving which fall on women (Finch and Groves, 1980, 1983; Walker, 1982; Land and Rose, 1985; Ungerson, 1987; Lewis and Meredith, 1988). A second theme of critical comment has been to point to the considerable sums of public expenditure which are saved by the largely unpaid and uncosted work of those involved in providing informal care and support for infirm or disabled relatives and friends (Rimmer, 1983). One recent estimate, using General Household Survey data, has put the value of the help given by those caring for more than 20 hours a week at between £11.5 and £15.2 billion (Family Policy Studies Centre, 1989).

Despite the increasing awareness of the role of carers and of their needs, the financial consequences of informal care-giving have remained largely unacknowledged in the development of community care policies. Thus, even though Griffiths was centrally concerned with the organisation and efficient use of financial resources to sustain community care, this concern was focused exclusively at an organisational rather than an individual level. His proposal for 'ring-fenced' funds for community care services was intended to safeguard the resources available to the main service-providing agencies, not to provide any additional financial support to individual carers. Indeed, Griffiths explicitly ruled out 'any extension of social services authorities' limited powers to make cash payments to individuals' (Griffiths, 1988, p. 14). Although the subsequent White Paper does refer to rising levels of social security expenditure on disabled people and carers, it makes no attempt to assess the adequacy or effectiveness of this provision and asserts simply that 'these figures demonstrate the Government's commitment to a fair and flexible system of support' (DH et al, 1989, p. 10).

Social security and carers

Social security policy-making over the past decade has also to a very large extent failed to address the issue of exactly how 'fair and flexible' the current system of financial support actually is. Indeed, it is arguable that the very invisibility of informal carers within this policy arena may have led almost inadvertently to an increase in their financial insecurity and risk of becoming impoverished.

Current social security provision for carers grew out of pressure to protect the incomes and retirement pensions of those whose full-time employment was ended prematurely by responsibility for the care of elderly relatives. Invalid care allowance (ICA) was first announced in a 1974 White Paper and introduced in 1976 for men and single women of working age. The benefit was eventually extended to married women in June 1986. Nevertheless ICA remains well below the level of both contributory national insurance benefits and the adult rate of income support; it carries a strict earnings limit; and is available only to working age carers who are spending at least 35 hours a week looking after a recipient of attendance allowance. Carers and their spouses who receive national insurance or means-tested benefits find that these are reduced, pound for pound, by the amount of ICA.

Many carers are therefore wholly or partially dependent on means-tested income support. However, carers were the only group of former long-term supplementary benefit claimants who did not receive a 'client group' premium when the new income support scheme was introduced in April 1988. This loss was not made up until October 1990, when a premium of £10 was introduced for income support claimants who are also in receipt of ICA. Because of the stringent eligibility conditions for ICA (particularly the exclusion of elderly carers), it is estimated that only 30,000 carers have benefited from the new premium.

In addition, from October 1988 the national insurance 'credits' for ICA recipients have no longer counted towards short-term national insurance benefits. This means that former carers may have no entitlement to unemployment benefit when they begin looking for paid work again after a period of full-time care-giving has come to an end – a measure which is estimated to affect 11,000 former carers (Hansard, 3.12.87, cols. 407–14).

Following the major social security changes in 1988, carers were promised that their social security needs would be considered as part of a forthcoming review of benefits for disabled people, to be carried out following the new OPCS surveys of disabled people (DHSS, 1985, para. 3.28). In the event, two changes affecting carers were announced some three months before the publication of the full disability benefits review, *The Way Ahead* (DSS, 1990a), which itself contained no additional proposals for carers' benefits. One of these changes was the additional £10 income support premium for those already in receipt of ICA (subsequently extended until 8 weeks after caring ceases); the other was an increase in the amount that ICA recipients can earn without affecting their benefit, from £12 to £20 a week (£30 from April 1991) (Hansard, 25.10.89, col. 844). These changes fell a long way short of what many carers' organisations had been hoping for: partly because the long-awaited review of disability benefits did not subsequently give any detailed consideration to the needs of carers; and partly because the two new measures would provide no additional help to the 13 per cent of adults over 65 estimated to be giving care (Green, 1988, p. 8). The review did not attempt to evaluate the coverage, adequacy or coherence of existing social security provision for carers, so it was not clear why these two particular measures had been selected as the highest priority for improving carers' benefits.

It was in fact left to the House of Commons Social Services Committee to provide a critical overview of this kind. In considering the implications of the Government's proposals for 'community care', the Committee addressed head-on the central issue of whether current arrangements provided carers with an adequate income. The Committee concluded that they did not:

> . . . the current social security system . . . is geared almost entirely to the partial replacement of earnings . . . it is difficult to argue that it effectively performs even this limited objective . . . the income replacement system deemed essential for pensioners and disabled people does not operate for carers. (House of Commons, 1990a, p. xxi)

The Social Services Committee report is important not simply because of the recommendations it makes. It may in future years come to be seen as a turning point because for the first time it brings together the two issues of community care and social security and begins to address the financial implications for those informal carers on whom the success of 'community care' depends. To paraphrase Sir Roy Griffiths' description of community care, the financial consequences of informal care-giving have been 'a poor relation; everybody's distant relative but nobody's baby' (Griffiths, 1988, p. iv).

The importance of costing care-giving

Research into the financial consequences of informal care-giving is, by and large, still at a fairly rudimentary stage. The reasons for this lie partly in the overwhelming concern of policy-makers, politicians and administrators alike about the *public* expenditure consequences of various policy options. Research has therefore tended to focus on the costs of various types and 'packages' of statutorily-funded residential and domiciliary services (see for example Wright, Cairns and Snell, 1981; Challis and Davis, 1980; Challis et al., 1983). While studies such as these are able to demonstrate that community care is both a cheaper and more effective alternative to residential or institutional care, this is because the costs of care which are being considered are by and large only the public expenditure costs: 'the costs to carers are being ignored' (Rimmer, 1983, p. 135). Yet this narrow focus on the *public* costs of care-giving can only be justified if it is assumed that informal care-giving, like other types of domestic and caring activities carried out within the private confines of the home and family, does not need to be or cannot be costed. Because it lies outside the sphere of formal economic activity and, moreover, because care-giving is assumed to be primarily a female activity, little value has traditionally been attached to it.

This assumption has come under considerable attack in recent years from a number of different sources. Perhaps the two most cogent (and influential) sets of arguments have stemmed first from analyses of the 'mixed economy of welfare' (Brenton, 1985; Glennester, 1985; Webb and Wistow, 1987); and, secondly, from feminist critiques of social policy research and practice. In particular, feminists have described the processes by which welfare is provided within the private domestic domain, pointing out that 'the family' is not a single undifferentiated unit but a complex organisation encompassing power relations, divisions of labour and unequal resource flows (Brannen and Wilson, 1987; Glendinning and Millar, 1987) and drawing attention to the especially heavy demands which are made on women to provide family or 'community' care (Graham, 1983, 1987; Finch and Groves, 1980, 1983; Joshi, 1987).

It is therefore less and less acceptable to consider simply the public expenditure implications of community care. It is increasingly clear that some very considerable private costs are also involved and, moreover, that these are distributed in a manner which is far from equal, especially so far as the costs which are borne by women and men are concerned. Furthermore, there is also increasing awareness that attempts in the short term to restrain public expenditure, by shifting the costs of care-giving into the private, informal or family sector, may have longer-term consequences which are far less desirable. For example, as the research reported in this monograph will indicate, the short-term financial impoverishment experienced by carers while engaged in intensive care-giving may also have longer-term public expenditure consequences, if they come to face their own old age with depleted savings and attenuated pension entitlements.

In the past such financial consequences may have been given relatively little importance, on the grounds that most informal care is carried out by married women whose position in relation to the labour market is marginal, but such assumptions no longer hold true. Over the last 40 years the proportion of married women in the labour force has increased substantially (Martin and Roberts, 1984; Lonsdale, 1987) and this trend is expected to increase yet further over the coming decade (Spence, 1990).

For reasons of both principle and pragmatism, therefore, it is increasingly impossible to ignore the costs of care-giving which currently fall on those individuals who provide substantial amounts of care on an informal basis to friends and relatives. In principle, such an oversight ignores the very unequal costs which are borne by some members of the 'community' on behalf of the 'community' as a whole. This in turn raises a fundamental question about the approach which should be taken by the state in relation to those costs. Should they be allowed to lie where they currently fall, with individual informal carers being expected to shoulder them relatively unaided as a necessary and expected consequence of the fulfilment of family obligations? Or should the state take a more active role in attempting to equalise the costs of caring, in the form of increased taxation and public expenditure on services and social security provision?

On a pragmatic level, overlooking the privately-borne costs of community care may prove a short-sighted, and false, economy. It may only increase the physical, emotional and social costs of informal caregiving, all of which may have substantial public policy implications in the longer term.

The aim of this monograph is to shed some light on these issues by describing the financial circumstances of a small group of carers who were providing help and support to a very infirm or severely disabled relative or friend, in order to put together a comprehensive picture of the financial consequences of giving care.

The carers

Focus of the study

The focus of the study was on the financial circumstances of working-age carers who were providing substantial amounts of help and support to a disabled person living in the same household. Parents caring for a disabled child or son or daughter disabled from birth were excluded (see Buckle, 1984; Baldwin, 1985; Hirst, 1985); as were men and women caring for a disabled spouse (see Parker, forthcoming). Carers were identified via respondents to the OPCS survey of disabled adults and through the users of a number of domiciliary and day care services in several different health and social services authorities. Interviews with a total of 30 carers were carried out. As the study was essentially exploratory, a semi-structured schedule was used. The interviews were tape-recorded and subsequently analysed to yield both qualitative and quantitative material.

The interviews were carried out during the summer of 1986, just before the government announced that ICA was to be extended to married women. However, most of the married women carers had already heard of the benefit and were able to discuss their likely eligibility for it. The interviews also preceded the major changes which took place in 1988 following the 1986 Social Security Act. The likely effects of these subsequent changes on carers and on the conclusions drawn from the study are described where appropriate.

Questions inevitably arise as to the representativeness of a sample of this size. The intention was to investigate particular aspects of the impact of caring, rather than carers in general, and the sample was deliberately selected in order to do that. There is nevertheless no reason to suppose that the carers identified by the OPCS disablement survey were in any way unrepresentative of carers with these particular characteristics. The subsequent use of a number of different services to supplement the sample was also intended to minimise the bias which may be associated with sampling from a single agency.

Although small, the study focused on a group of carers whose circumstances are a clear priority for policy-makers. First, they were caring for people who needed a good deal of help. Secondly, because they were same-household carers, their lives were likely to be more severely affected by the demands of caring. Thirdly, because the carers in this study were of working age, the financial impact of caring was likely to be particularly significant.

The carers in the study

The 29 households in this study contained a total of 30 carers. In most instances it was possible to carry out an interview with one 'main' or primary carer, apart from one household in which an unmarried brother and sister shared equally in the supervision and physical care of their elderly father.

In six of the households, the disabled person had recently ceased living with the carer because s/he had died (three cases), had been admitted permanently to residential care (two cases), or had gone to live with other relatives (one case). In these instances, information was collected about the situation during the previous year.

Of the 30 carers, 23 were looking after their mothers, three their fathers, one a mother-in-law, one a father-in-law, one an adult daughter and one a friend. No carer was currently looking after more than one severely disabled person, although several carers had previously supported both their ageing parents.

Seven of the carers were men, of whom five had never married, one was divorced and one currently married. The five single men were unmarried sons who had continued living in the family home and had begun to care for an elderly parent when this became necessary. The divorced male carer had also lived with his parents for the whole of his adult life apart from a brief marriage. The one married man was caring for his father who had Parkinson's Disease; he was the only person in the family from whom his father would accept help with personal care.

Of the 23 female carers a similarly high proportion – ten in all – were not currently married. Seven had never married and remained living with their parent(s) throughout their adult lives. Almost all of these 'never married' daughters were in their late forties and fifties, and all were caring for elderly parents. The one single woman in the study who did not fit this 'unmarried daughter' pattern was in her mid-twenties, living with and caring for a disabled female friend.

The remaining three women who were not currently married were also all in their late forties to mid-fifties. Two were widowed and one divorced. The latter's divorce and the death of one of the widows' husbands had taken place long before their elderly parents had begun to need a substantial amount of care, so both had effectively been 'single' at the time. The death of the other widowed woman's husband had virtually coincided with the death of the two unmarried brothers who had been living with and looking after their mother. The mother therefore moved to live with her newly-widowed daughter.

The age range of the 13 married women carers was much wider, from thirty to sixty, although the majority were in their mid-forties or older. Most were caring for elderly parents, especially their own mothers, apart from one woman looking after a daughter who had been partially paralysed 12 years earlier at the age of 16.

Three features of this small group of carers warrant particular comment. The first is their age distribution, particularly noticeable among the female carers; two-thirds of the 23 women were aged between 45 and 64. This is consistent with the national picture that the heaviest and most common caring responsibilities tend to affect working-age women carers towards the end of their working lives (Green, 1988, pp. 8–9).

Secondly, the vast majority of the carers, both male and female, were looking after relatives with whom they had primary kin relationships – their own mothers, fathers or daughter. Only three were caring for less closely related kin – a mother-in-law, father-in-law and a friend. Again this is consistent with national surveys, which show that more than nine out of ten carers who are living in the same household as the person they are caring for are looking after a close relative or in-law (Green, 1988, p. 16).

The third interesting feature of the sample is the relatively high proportion of single (i.e. never married) carers – over a third of the total sample, and five out of seven of the male carers. Again this is consistent with national figures. The 1985 GHS found particularly heavy caring responsibilities among single people in the 45–64 age group (Green, 1988, p. 10).

Thirteen carers (nine unmarried and four who were widowed or divorced) lived in two-adult households alone with the cared-for person. Six carers lived in three-adult households. These included the unmarried sister and brother who jointly shared their father's care and a third unmarried carer who also lived with a brother as well as their mother. The remaining three carers in three-person households were all older married women living with their husbands and the cared-for person, with adult children now living away from home. Five carers lived in four-person households, usually consisting of themselves, their spouse and one remaining adult non-dependent child, as well as the person being cared for. Finally, six carers lived in five-person households. These carers were on the whole younger, with a combination of dependent and non-dependent children living at home with them, a spouse and the disabled person.

Over a third of the carers lived in households in which they, their spouse or a child also had a longstanding health problem, illness or disability. In six of these 12 households it was the health of other household members which was not good, but in nine households carers also mentioned health problems of their own. Three of these carers suffered from serious back and other muscular problems as a result of the lifting which they had to do.

The people receiving care

The majority of the people receiving care were elderly. Only four of the 29 were aged 60 or under, while 22 were over 70 years old, 13 of them aged 80 and over. The majority were also female; women outnumbered men by about ten to one. The illnesses and disabling conditions from which they suffered were therefore those closely associated with advancing age: circulatory disorders, arthritis and, in particular, senile dementia. Over half had more than one disorder – several had three or four complaints.

On the whole, the onset of these health problems or disabilities was relatively recent; over the sample as a whole, the average length of time since the symptoms had first begun to appear or the disability had occurred was almost 9 years and for more than a third (12) this had been within the past five years. The relatively recent onset of these disabling conditions, combined with the current severe impairments of the people receiving care, suggests that many had apparently deteriorated quite rapidly. Only three were reported to have improved since they first became disabled; all had experienced a disabling physical trauma from which they had subsequently regained some motor functions.

All of the people receiving care had impaired mobility. Over two-thirds were unable to walk at all or could only manage a few steps around the house with considerable support. Two-thirds suffered from some incontinence, including five who were doubly incontinent.

All the disabled people needed help with personal care activities, or constant supervision to avoid danger. Over half were reported to have some communication problems, usually because of severe short-term memory loss, and were considered by their carers to be frequently confused about the time or about who people were.

Around a third could not be left alone in the house at all during the day or during the evening, and a further third could only be left for up to an hour. Of those who could not be left alone in the house at all, half could not be left alone in the sitting room or bedroom for more than an hour or so during the daytime or evening.

Many carers therefore felt that they themselves could only be away from the house for very short periods when their disabled relative was at home. For a third the maximum time away was two hours, and over half the sample felt unable to be away for more than four hours. Opportunities to get out without the disabled person tended to be restricted mainly to the mornings or afternoons, between mealtimes.

Just under half (13) of the cared-for people woke regularly or needed attention during the night. The responsibility for providing this tended to lie with the main carer, even in those households where there were also other people. At the most extreme, six carers found themselves woken several times each night because of their relative's restlessness, incontinence or need for help with toileting.

Three case studies

Case study one

Ms Cox[1] *was in her fifties and lived with her husband, a 20-year old daughter who was in full-time employment, and her mother. Ms Cox's mother's senile dementia had begun three years earlier. After a rapid deterioration, which included a period of aggression and violence, she was now completely dependent physically, unable to stand, doubly incontinent and with no effective communication. She had previously lived ten doors away from Ms Cox and had moved to live with her two and a half years ago, after a period in a nursing home and hospital.*

Ms Cox worked full time as a health visitor and school nurse. She had had to forego further training opportunities because of caring for her mother, which had restricted her promotion prospects. Her husband was a shop manager. While Ms Cox was at work her former domestic help came in to look after her mother and Mr Cox also helped on his day off each week. The cost of this additional substitute care was met from Ms Cox's mother's income – retirement pension and higher rate attendance allowance. Ms Cox therefore had to meet most of her mother's daily living expenses plus a number of additional expenses – heating, laundry, special clothing that was easier to put on and take off, extra toiletries, and any personal items her mother needed – from her own and her husband's income. Although Ms Cox had access to all

---

[1] All names have been changed to preserve anonymity.

her mother's financial resources (she had taken Power of Attorney over her mother's affairs), these still fell far short of her mother's actual needs. Ms Cox was nevertheless determined to continue working full time and caring for her mother for as long as her own physical health would permit (both she and her husband had suffered physical problems caused by lifting her mother).

Case study two

Mr Parks *was a single man aged 33. He had always lived with his mother, who was now 65 and had suffered from multiple sclerosis for the previous 20 years. She was unable to walk or stand and needed considerable help with toileting, which her son provided.*

Mr Parks had taken over looking after his mother when his father died. He had then been working as the manager of a menswear shop. After his father's death he continued to work full time for a year. He then negotiated a switch to part-time work, at the same hourly rate of pay. However even this proved too difficult so after five years he gave up his job altogether and for the past six months had received invalid care allowance (see Chapter 6). Mr Parks was therefore substantially dependent financially on his mother. She received retirement and graduated pensions, mobility and higher rate attendance allowances. Their pooled incomes nevertheless also had to cover extra spending on the special diet, laundry, toiletries, transport and house redecoration which Mr Parks' mother's disability necessitated. His mother's savings also financed any repairs or new furniture for their home.

Mr Parks was painfully aware of his own poverty and the vulnerability of being dependent on his mother for financial support, although in the long term he hoped to be able to return to paid work. He was also uncertain about his ability to carry on looking after his mother if she began to need a great deal of night-time care or experience severe pain. Given his present precarious financial situation, the possibility that she might need residential care caused him considerable worry.

Case study three

Ms Tree *was a single woman aged 51, who lived with her unmarried brother aged 56 and their 89-year old mother. Ms Tree's mother had begun to suffer from senile dementia four years ago and had deteriorated rapidly during two bouts of serious illness. She was now bedridden, incontinent, and was not able to communicate. She could only be left alone in the house for a few minutes, if she was in bed asleep. Ms Tree provided most of her mother's personal care, although her brother and a number of other siblings sat with her while Ms Tree was at work. Indeed, Ms Tree had chosen to take over washing her mother each morning from the community nurse, so that she could maintain a predictable routine and ensure that all her mother's personal care would be completed by the time she went to work at lunchtime.*

Ms Tree had worked full time for the past 16 years as a supervisor for a major chain store firm. When her mother first became ill she took several months off work, but was then offered the opportunity of reducing her job to part-time hours with the promise of a return to full-time work when her circumstances permitted. Although still earning the same hourly rate of pay, Ms Tree estimated that she had lost approximately £8,000 in the two years up to 1986. Her brother, a self-employed craftsman, also lost earnings because he regularly came home early to sit with their mother.

Ms Tree estimated that because of her mother's illness their heating bills had doubled, there was much more spending on laundry and extra bedding, and she also bought substantially more cleaning materials and toiletries. As a household, Ms Tree, her brother and her mother effectively pooled most of their resources. Ms Tree's mother's income (retirement pension and higher rate attendance allowance) was split entirely between the housekeeping, for which Ms Tree was responsible, and the fuel and rates bills, which her brother dealt with. Ms Tree felt that she and her brother were to some extent subsidising their mother – her own income would not, she felt, have covered all her extra needs and especially not the extra heating. Nevertheless she regarded these subsidies, and her own reduced income, as a fair exchange for the home which her mother had continued to provide for her. As she had not had to bear the costs of setting up home on her own, she felt able to bear these more recent financial losses.

Becoming a carer: anticipating the financial consequences

While other studies (Qureshi and Walker, 1989; Wenger, 1984) have explored the patterns of decision-making within extended family networks about the assumption of responsibility for the care of an elderly relative, other issues were of more concern here. To what extent had carers been aware of the possible financial implications of providing a substantial amount of care; and to what extent had any such knowledge – or the lack of it – influenced their behaviour?

Care-giving and household formation

Thirteen of the 30 carers had been living with the disabled person since birth. Most were unmarried women and men who had never left the parental home; the thirteenth was a woman whose daughter had not moved away from home following her disablement at the age of 16. For only three of this group of carers had an original intention to move away from home been disrupted by the onset of the disabled person's need for care. Although all of these three carers had subsequently experienced negative effects on their careers, employment or earnings as a result of the day-to-day constraints imposed by caring, these could not be attributed specifically to the failure to move out of the parental home or to another area in search of a better job, for example.

None of these three carers had had any pressure placed on them by doctors, social workers or other professionals to change their plans and stay at home to look after their relatives; the decision had been made entirely within the context of the family and the perceived availability of other family members:

> I've got a couple of sisters. I suppose – they're both married and maybe they didn't want her.
> (Mr Church, whose mother had a number of disabling conditions)

None of the remaining ten carers who had shared a household with the disabled person since birth had had any plans to leave home or move away which had been frustrated by becoming a carer.

A second group of carers consisted of four who had not always lived with the disabled person, but who had begun to do so well before the latter began to need a great deal of help. Their reasons for beginning to live together were varied. Two, Ms Chester and Ms Bell, had returned to live with their mothers because both of them had needed accommodation when a residential job and marriage respectively had ended. Ms Lord's mother and Mr Boot's father on the other hand had come to live with them some years earlier following the death of their respective spouses. Although neither parent had been in good health at the time, neither had then needed the amount of help and supervision which they now did. For these four carers, because the decision to live together was not prompted by the pressing care needs of the elderly relative, few financial or other consequences had been anticipated at the time.

However, for a third, large, group of carers, the possible financial consequences were of far greater relevance. All of these carers had formed joint households specifically for the purpose of providing care, either in response to a gradual deterioration in the disabled person's condition or after an accident or illness:

> . . . the neighbours started to notice that she was doing unusual things and they started to be concerned about her . . . She'd turn the gas fire on and leave it turned on without lighting it. She'd turned the gas cooker on and forgotten . . . and was burning pans . . . She'd locked herself out of the house on more than one occasion . . . She'd been for her pension and we couldn't find her money anywhere, and by sheer fluke I looked under the stairs where she kept her old newspapers, and found £5 notes between the layers of newspapers that she was ready to throw out.
> (Ms Franks, whose mother had senile dementia)

> [When mother had her first stroke] she was on the floor all night and we got to know because the neighbours next door found her and that's how she ended up in hospital . . . That was the only way they would release her from hospital, when she asked me to take her in.
> (Ms Harris, who had looked after her mother for the past ten years)

In the majority of these instances the disabled or elderly people had given up their own homes and moved to live with their carers and – because all but two of these carers were married daughters or daughters-in-law – their sons (-in-law) and sometimes grandchildren as well. The two exceptions were Ms Peel and her friend Jenny, who had *both* moved into a ground-floor housing association flat following the latter's discharge from a Spinal Injuries Unit; and Ms Dale and her family who themselves moved to live with her mother:

> We had our own house. Then mum had her stroke and we decided that we wanted to look after her . . . she was living here on her own. [When she came out of hospital] we'd already moved in. We moved the end of December, sold our house and moved in here. She came out of hospital about Easter time.

About half of the disabled people who moved from their own homes to live with their carers left behind rented accommodation, so no major sums of money were released by the sale of their homes. The remainder sold their homes and realised an often substantial amount of money which would, in the normal course of events, have eventually been inheritied by children and/or grandchildren. Some of the elderly people disposed of the capital in ways which reflected this pattern or which seemed to indicate that normal inheritance patterns would be followed in the future: they invested the money in trust for their grandchildren; shared it equally between all their children (including the carer); or simply put it into their building society or bank account.

In only two instances was the capital used in ways which explicitly recognised and took account of the disabled person's need for additional care during the remainder of their life:

> My mother said 'You have it' and I thought 'Yes, I will' because she was getting less able to sign her name for her pension so I thought this would be sensible, to put it to one side . . . and leave it for her in case we ever needed for example to put her into a private home . . . so we put it in a building society.
> (Ms Franks, whose mother had severe dementia)

After Ms Dale's mother's stroke, she had signed over the ownership of her house, which had no outstanding mortgage on it, to her daughter and son-in-law. Ms and Mr Dale had then used some of the capital from the sale of their house to build and equip a ground-floor bedroom and bathrooom extension to Ms Dale's mother's house, to which they then moved.

Anticipating the financial effects

Deciding to form a joint household with a disabled or elderly relative for the purposes of providing care marked a definitive stage in the process of becoming a carer. To what extent did these carers take the possible financial consequences into account?

Only a quarter of those carers who had brought the disabled person to live with them had expected that this might affect their employment, then or in the future:

> I were applying for jobs . . . I'd just got [my daughter] into school . . . I said to the doctor 'Well that's the end of that then'. 'Do you work?' he said. I said 'No and I aren't going to now, am I?'
> (*Ms Johnson, whose mother had Alzheimer's disease*)

The remaining carers were at the time either not actively seeking work, did not define themselves as potential members of the labour market, or did not anticipate any impact on their employment – some of them erroneously because they had not expected the disabled person's need for care to be so demanding, to last so long, or to be so unsupported by statutory services:

> I hadn't anticipated giving up work, I thought I could manage the three hours. But the thing was . . . in the summer days she came out to meet me, her petticoat round her top. She'd got changed during the afternoon. My heart nearly broke when I saw her . . . and then twice she ran after me as I was getting on the bus – didn't want me to go. The time had come to stop work.
> (*Ms Grey, who had given up her job as a child welfare clinic clerical officer several months after her mother came to live with her*)

Similarly, virtually none of these 13 carers had anticipated any additional financial expenses (over and above these of simply having an extra person in the household). Again, they sometimes recognised with hindsight that this assumption had been erroneous:

> We thought that everything would even itself out . . . but having said that, we obviously have increased fuel bills.
> (*Ms Dale, whose family moved to live in her mother's house after the latter's stroke*)

> It is definitely more expensive, but I never thought – I mean, I'd never had a 'phone before, and this stupid heating, you have to have it on all the time – just basic running costs.
> (*Ms Peel, who moved into a new flat to care for her friend Jenny, who had suffered a spinal injury in a road accident*)

Only three carers had made any enquiries about the social security benefits to which they or their disabled relatives might be entitled were they to live together, but in no case had the knowledge of potential benefit eligibility been a factor in the decision to live together.

On the other hand, none of the carers had foreseen any financial advantages for themselves and their families either. The advantages which they did foresee were essentially non-material ones; it would be easier from a practical point of view to live with the disabled person than to continue providing high levels of support from a separate household:

> The advantages were that I wouldn't be flying up and down the road, and that me and me husband were at home in the middle of the evenings rather than going and sitting down there.
> (*Ms Johnson, whose mother had dementia*)

However, carers did anticipate some material advantages for the disabled person as a result of living together, especially the better standard of living and quality of care which s/he would enjoy, rather than living on her own or in an institutional setting:

> The material comfort she could have at home and the individual care she could have at home, instead of being one of 28, 30; peace and quiet instead of being on a hospital ward.
> (*Ms Cox, whose mother had severe dementia*)

> She would have her family, she would have comfort . . . her meals regularly, plus we could take her out, there were things we could do for her.
> (*Ms McFee, whose mother had moved from London to live with her in Yorkshire*)

None of the carers had therefore apparently given much prior consideration to the possible financial consequences of living with and caring for their disabled relatives. The few who had, had either been concerned only with the potential advantages and benefits for the disabled person or had been more than willing to carry whatever financial costs would fall on them, because of their feelings towards the disabled person:

> Money doesn't come into it with anything for me. I'm not bothered about money . . . I just made sure that's what me mother really wanted.
> (*Ms Harris, widow aged 47, whose mother had come to live with her following a stroke 10 years ago*)

However, before we conclude that financial considerations do not play any part in the decision to live with and care for a severely disabled person, it is important to remember that we have only half the picture from this study. We as yet know nothing about those people with a relative or friend needing a substantial amount of care who decided that they do not or cannot provide that in the context of a shared household. Nor do we know anything about the reasons on which they might base that decision. It may well be that such potential carers *do* take careful account of the financial consequences of such a move, and decide that the extra costs or possible damage to their employment prospects which might be involved would be too great.

Incomes and other resources of the disabled people

Information on the incomes and other resources of the disabled people is important for three reasons. First, assessments of the financial consequences of care-giving must take place within the context of the household's overall financial resources. Secondly, the nature of the financial consequences for carers depended very much on the *relative* income levels of the carer and disabled person. Thirdly, carers' own incomes were often determined at least in part by those of the disabled person, particularly the latter's receipt of attendance allowance.

Income maintenance benefits

None of the 29 disabled people had any earnings. The majority (25) received most of their weekly income in the form of a state retirement pension. Three of these elderly people also received a small gradu-ated state pension, but in no instance was this more than £5.

The four disabled people who did not depend for most of their basic weekly income on a state retirement pension included the three who were below retirement age. Ms Peel's friend Jenny, aged 31, received national insurance invalidity pension plus the highest age-related invalidity allowance; Ms Flaxman's daughter Helen, aged 28, received severe disablement allowance 'topped up' by supplementary benefit; and Ms Kahn's mother, aged 41, received a national insurance widow's pension, again 'topped up' by supplementary benefit. The fourth non-recipient of retirement pension was Ms McFee's mother, aged 60, who had been separated from her husband and who apparently had no entitlement to national insurance benefits through either her own or her ex-husband's contributions. She therefore received all her income from means-tested supplementary benefit.

Only eight of the 29 disabled people had occupational pensions. The levels of these varied considerably, ranging from £6 to £38 a week (only 4 had occupational pensions over £15 a week).

Only seven of the disabled people received any supplementary benefit – all, apart from Ms McFee's mother, in addition to another non-means-tested contributory or non-contributory benefit. Six of these seven SB recipients received at least one weekly additional requirement on top of their basic weekly benefit, most commonly for heating, extra laundry and special diets.

Three main factors determined the disabled people's potential eligibility for supplementary benefit in this pre-1988 study. First, seven disabled people with savings over £3,000 were completely ineligible for supplementary benefit:

> Mum can't get supplementary benefit because the house price went into her bank account.
> (*Ms Cox, whose mother's house had been sold when she moved to live with her daughter*)

Secondly, those disabled people who were deemed to be non-householders had substantially lower basic supplementary benefit entitlements than either single or joint householders:

> We applied [for supplementary benefit] when mother was still at [her former] home, for about two months before she came to live with me . . . It only made a difference of about £3 a week, but the things that she could get without paying for, should she need . . . Of course she lost all that as soon as she came to live with us.
> (*Ms Johnson, married woman with two young children, caring for her mother who had senile dementia*)

Thirdly, the occupational pensions received by some of the disabled people rendered their income levels too high to qualify for supplementary benefit.

This overwhelming reliance on statutory benefits meant that only two of the disabled people in this study had weekly incomes which were equivalent to at least 140 per cent of what would have been their notional supplementary benefit entitlement. This picture appears to be broadly consistent with that found by the national OPCS survey (Martin and White, 1988). With the April 1988 social security changes, especially the raising of the capital cut-off to £6000 and the removal of the different benefit rates for householders and non-householders, it is possible that the benefit entitlements of disabled elderly people living in circumstances similar to those in this study may have been increased as a consequence of the change from supplementary benefit to income support. Nevertheless their total weekly income levels, relative to both non-disabled and non-elderly people, would on the whole have remained low.

Disability benefits

Two social security benefits are also available to help meet the additional costs of disability. Neither is itself means-tested, or taken into account in income assessments for other means-tested benefits. The attendance allowance is payable to those who need substantial or repeated help with personal care or supervision to avoid danger; the mobility allowance to those who become unable or virtually unable to walk while of working age.

All but seven of the cared-for people were receiving at least one of these disability benefits. Twelve received attendance allowance at the higher rate, ten received the lower rate and six received mobility allowance.

Mobility allowance is payable only to those who develop severe locomotor disabilities before the age of 65. There was no evidence of non-take up of this benefit; all the disabled people under 65 with severe locomotor problems were receiving it. The remainder had been too old when they first became disabled to claim it.

There was, however, evidence that some of the disabled people who were not receiving attendance allowance might have been eligible for it, or had experienced other problems in establishing their eligibility. The attendance allowance is of considerable importance because of the role which it plays as a 'passport' to other benefits, both for the disabled person and her/his carer. Since April 1988, attendance allowance has been one of the 'passporting' benefits which entitles income support claimants under 60 to a disability premium and those over 60 to a higher pension premium. Attendance allowance receipt also exempts a carer from signing on as available for work as a condition of receiving income support and is one of the major qualifying conditions to be met before a carer can receive invalid care allowance and, since 1990, the income support carer's premium.

The attendance allowance was also important because, as other studies have shown (see Horton and Berthoud, 1990), it played a crucial role in helping to meet the extra costs of disability. In the absence of the allowance, these costs tended to fall on their carers:

> There was a time when we were subsidising him, but we're not now because . . . we learnt [from the OPCS survey interviewer] that we would possibly be eligible for attendance allowance, which we didn't know about . . . Up until getting this attendance allowance he was giving me £30 a week, but then when he got the attendance allowance he gave that to me.
> (*Ms Rivers, married woman, looking after her father-in-law*)

Seven disabled people were not receiving attendance allowance although four of them undoubtedly satisfied at least one of the benefit's attendance or supervision criteria. Some still had to wait to complete the initial six-month qualifying period before applying:

> I don't know what you've got to have before you can get it . . . We applied . . . second of June I think, then we got a letter from Blackpool saying they couldn't decide yet, so she's going to have to have another medical, beginning of December, before me mother can get the attendance allowance.
> (*Ms Halifax, whose mother was seriously incapacitated by lung cancer*)

Some carers had been misinformed or were simply unaware of their relatives' potential eligibility, though they would undoubtedly have qualified:

> I just assumed that because my brother was at home that we wouldn't come under it. And then I went to the carers' meeting [at the Day Centre] and there was somebody there from CAB and they said 'You should have been getting it ages ago'.
> (*Ms Carlisle, main carer of her mother, who had senile dementia*)

> You can't have attendance allowance if you're taken away every day. I did enquire about it and they said that with them taking her onto the [Day Hospital] Ward Monday, Tuesday, Wednesday, Thursday, Friday, in fact I wasn't eligible for the attendance allowance . . . It was the DHSS told me.
> (*Mr Dawn, whose mother had severe senile dementia*)

Two more non-recipients had not heard of attendance allowance, according to their carers. However, it is possible that they would not have qualified for the attendance allowance had they applied, as with Ms Bell's mother (the seventh non-recipient), whose application had been unsuccessful even after a review assisted by the local Citizens Advice Bureau.

In total, only two out of this sample of 29 severely disabled people appeared to meet all the eligibility criteria for attendance allowance but had nevertheless not claimed it. This does, not however, include another aspect of underclaiming, of which there was considerable evidence. Only nine of the 22 current recipients of attendance allowance had apparently claimed it as soon as they became eligible; the remaining 13 had, according to their carers, probably been eligible for some years before they eventually received it. There seemed to be a number of reasons for these delays. First, none of the disabled or elderly people who had previously been living on their own had applied for the allowance before they had moved to live with their carers, however disabled they had been and however much domiciliary help and support they had previously been receiving from statutory and family sources. Secondly, some carers had experienced real doubts about their relatives' eligibility, particularly when there was some uncertainty about their prognosis:

> No we didn't [apply as soon as we learnt about the attendance allowance] because when we read the leaflet it said it can take as long as three months to – before anybody actually comes to see you. It's quite a long process and right at the beginning she was so ill we didn't think she was going to live three months so we felt there was no point to it.
> (*Ms Tree, whose mother had senile dementia*)

Thirdly, there was difficulty in assessing the eligibility of elderly people whose own estimations of their abilities were far from realistic:

> It was when mother first came here and I asked straight away, but she didn't get it straight away because she put her foot in it. She kept telling them about all the things she could do. And I explained to the doctor . . . 'She may be telling you all this but she can't do it' . . . It was a couple of years, three years after before I tried again.
> (*Ms Harris, whose mother had had a serious stroke*)

The disabled people's savings and other capital resources

Only seven of the disabled people had savings of more than £3,000 (then the capital cut-off for supplementary benefit entitlement). However, only one of these regularly used the interest generated by her savings to supplement her income and improve the living standards of herself and her carer:

> She [mother] put [the money left by my father] in a high investment account and it brings her so much every six months. Well that money, the interest, she uses for spending on the house . . . We have spent a bit on the house lately, but most things have been done now . . .
> (*Mr Parks, whose mother suffered from multiple sclerosis*)

Was any of the capital (as distinct from the interest which it generated) used to improve the carers' quality of life or to help offset some of the costs of care which were experienced?

Only two carers and their disabled relatives were retaining the latter's savings wholly intact and anticipated continuing to do so in the future. The capital of the remaining five was currently or soon to be drawn on. Two carers had drawn on their relatives' savings in ways which improved their own living standards, while two other carers anticipated having to draw on the disabled person's savings in the near future, in both instances to help pay for respite or residential care.

To summarise, only a quarter of the disabled people had any substantial savings. An even smaller proportion – only one in seven – of carers currently used or planned to use their relatives' savings in ways which benefited them or contributed towards the cost of care-giving.

Even though in these few instances the disabled person's savings were helping to maintain the living standards and quality of life of their carers, it is nevertheless important to remember that this was almost certainly at the cost of the carers' own long-term inheritance. Resources which may have been available in the future to ease carers back into paid work after they had ceased providing care, or to maintain them in their own old age were being spent to alleviate the current impact of caring. However, for the majority of carers this potential choice between current and deferred spending was entirely absent – their relatives simply did not have the levels of savings which might have made a difference, either now or in the future.

Carers' incomes I: the impact of giving care on employment and earnings

Providing care for a disabled or elderly person clearly has implications for carers' employment and earnings. For example, 12 per cent of employed women and nearly a third (29 per cent) of non-employed women in the 1980 Women and Employment Survey who were caring for a disabled or elderly person reported restrictions on their employment opportunities (Martin and Roberts, 1984, p. 113). Studies of specific groups of carers – the parents of disabled children (Baldwin, 1985; Hirst, 1985), the sons and daughters of frail elderly people (Nissel and Bonnerjea, 1983; Wright, 1986) – have documented these effects in more detail.

Nevertheless it is also clear that combining paid employment and care-giving is the rule rather than the exception. The 1985 General Household Survey found that 43 per cent of working age carers who were spending at least 20 hours a week caring nevertheless had some paid employment, 26 per cent of them full-time and 17 per cent part-time. As in the general population, female carers were much more likely than male carers to be working part-time (Green, 1988, p. 23). However, an association between lower rates of labour market participation and care-giving may not be because caring responsibilities have led to a withdrawal from the labour market, but because people who are not currently economically active are more likely to take on major caring responsibilities than those currently in paid work.

Insights into the long-term impact of caring on employment are also very limited. In the absence of longitudinal research, this means exploring in detail carers' employment histories, their employment situation at the time they began providing substantial amounts of care, the changes which subsequently took place, changes which carers anticipate making in the future and details of the immediate and longer-term financial consequences of any such changes.

Although much of the interest in the relationship between care-giving and paid work has centred on the economic 'opportunity costs' of caring, employment also has important non-material benefits. It is valued for the status and sense of identity it confers, both inside and outside the home, and for the social contacts it guarantees. The loss of these non-material benefits because of heavy caring commitments can be felt as keenly by women as it is conventionally assumed to affect men (Nissel and Bonnerjea, 1983). This indicates the attention which needs to be given to the circumstances in which paid employment and care-giving are combined and the factors which facilitate this.

Sex, marital status and employment patterns

The employment histories and current circumstances of the 30 carers in this study were complex. The table below shows their current employment status by sex and marital status.

Employment Status, Sex and Marital Status of Carers

	Men	Married women	Single, widowed, divorced women
Working: full-time	3	3	–
part-time/casual	–	4	4
Retired	–	1	–
Registered unemployed	2	–	2
Not economically active	2	5	4
Total	7	13	10

(The category of 'not economically active' includes those carers who were not registering as available for work because of their caring activities. The four carers who were still registering for work may also have been able to cease registering because of their caring responsibilities.)

Significantly, the male carers were as likely as the female carers not to be in paid work. Equally significant was the fact that among the female carers, those who were currently married and therefore had a second wage coming into the household to fall back on, were as likely to be in paid employment as the single women who had no other means of support. Less surprising was the fact that the female carers, whatever their marital status, appeared to have more opportunities than their male counterparts for part-time or casual paid work.

There were no clear differences between the male and female carers, nor between those who were single and married, in their levels of skills, qualifications or subsequent employment histories. The following examples illustrate the diverse patterns:

Mr Boot, *the one married male carer in the study, had left school at 15 and continued his education at nightschool. His first job had been in joinery, from which he had subsequently moved to shoe-repairing and had eventually managed a shoe shop. He had then worked for the Electricity Board; then for a firm of auto-electrical agents; and for the past ten years had run his own wholesale business, selling electrical components to car repair garages.*

Ms Chester, *aged 57, was unmarried. She had left school at 14 and become a receptionist to an eye specialist, moving to become his live-in housekeeper and nurse his sick wife. Following both their deaths, she obtained another housekeeping job; this was followed by a period of part-time office cleaning before her mother became too frail to be left alone and she stopped work altogether.*

Ms Franks, *married with a 19–year old son at university, had obtained her teaching certificate at the age of 20. She had taken four years off from teaching when her son was born, but had returned to part-time and then full-time teaching. Now at 49 she was the head teacher of a primary school with a strong commitment to maintaining her career, despite caring for her mother with severe senile dementia for the last seven years.*

The only clear pattern to emerge from the employment histories of these 30 carers was the consistency with which those women who had had children had withdrawn temporarily from the labour market. However, childbearing was not the only reason for which carers had experienced earlier breaks in their paid work. Four had been made redundant or become unemployed during the period immediately before their relatives had begun to need a great deal of care, and three others had had earlier periods out of work caring for sick or elderly relatives, although only Ms Bryan considered that this earlier break had had adverse consequences:

> . . . I went to a firm called ABC where I was in charge of the office; I had quite a good job there. I stayed there seven years then I did leave because my mother wasn't very well. I very foolishly gave my job up altogether thinking I could get a part-time job . . . Unfortunately I didn't get a job and I was at home twelve months doing nothing . . . [Then I went to] the Town Hall . . . as a temporary clerk part-time.

Carers currently in paid work

Six carers were currently in full-time employment. Three were married women, employed as a primary school head teacher, a school nurse/health visitor and a staff nurse in a mental handicap hospital. The rest were men. Two, both unmarried, worked respectively as a self-employed pharmacist and a production operative in a bacon processing factory; Mr Boot, as already described, was also self-employed, as an auto-electric wholesaler.

Six carers, all women, were currently employed part-time in skilled manual and clerical occupations. Two more women worked on a casual basis, one doing temporary clerical work and one as a relief nursery nurse.

Almost half of this small sample of carers was therefore currently employed, in spite of their very heavy caring commitments. However most had experienced restrictions on their employment in the past; knew their future employment opportunities to be limited; or were currently managing to retain their employment only at considerable financial (and sometimes emotional) cost.

Restrictions experienced by employed carers

Only three of the 14 employed carers had begun their current jobs *since* starting to provide a substantial amount of care and all considered that their choice of new employment had been severely limited:

> If me mother hadn't been ill, I could have taken a full-time job. But now that she is ill I can only work part-time and only in [this town] . . . it could only be afternoons now.
> (*Ms Halifax, doing clerical work on a casual basis*)

Within their current jobs, over half the employed carers experienced restrictions on their hours of work. These invariably arose because carers could not leave their relatives alone for long; because substitute care was not available at particular times of the day, or for particular caring tasks; or because the cost of buying (additional) private substitute care would have been prohibitively expensive, given their levels of income.

Most commonly, carers had had to cut their hours of work. Ms Tree had been forced to reduce her full-time job as a chain store supervisor to half days only:

> I *have* to be here in a morning . . . because that's the biggest strain, getting her up in the morning and the washing and changing . . . I should really be there [at work] full-time. If they hadn't let me work

half days I don't know what I'd have done, that would have been very difficult.

Carers in full-time paid work, particularly those in self-employment, had also had to cut down their hours. Shift work and overtime opportunities had also been affected:

> I couldn't cope with never knowing when I was going to be there – you had to wait till the rota was up to see which days you'd be working . . . I was doing 20 hours. When the job was reviewed because of the situation I was in, I reduced it to 14 and regular hours, so that I could go at nine and finish at four [two days a week].
> (*Ms Rivers, nursing auxiliary in a maternity hospital*)

> Since me dad's been home I've not done any overtime. When it has been [available] I've had to turn round and say 'No'.
> (*Mr Harvester, production worker in bacon processing factory*)

Other carers felt unable to take the opportunities which were available to work longer than their current limited hours:

> If I didn't have me mother I could have more hours, if I had no ties. But I'm at work and I'm thinking 'I've got to get back'. Probably I'd have had to give some hours up if I hadn't had [neighbour] next door [to check on mother].
> (*Ms Lincoln, working part-time as a home help*)

Four of the employed carers had been unable to undertake further training which would have enhanced their future job prospects:

> I've been asked if I wanted to do a nurse's training but I wouldn't want to put the amount of hours and commitment into it – I couldn't, I couldn't.
> (*Ms Rivers, nursing auxiliary in a maternity hospital*)

Almost half of the employed carers considered that they had actually lost pay because of care-giving, because they had had to change jobs, reduce their hours of work or overtime, or take time off in emergencies. For example, Ms Dale, until two and a half years ago earning £30 a week as a care assistant, now took just £60 a month from her husband's business for doing the accounts; Mr Boot thought that his auto-electric wholesale business was being put at risk because of the time he spent looking after his father; and Ms Tree had changed from full- to part-time work:

> I reckon over the past two years I've probably lost about £8,000 with being at home, in lost earnings . . . Compared to the rest of the family, I've lost a lot more than the rest of them . . . financially.

Managing employment and care-giving

How did carers manage to combine paid work with caring? What arrangements did they make while they were at work; how satisfactory and reliable were these; and what, if any, were the financial consequences of these arrangements?

Only two of the disabled people were able to be left at home with no substitute care arrangements at all while their carers were at work. Three more carers relied entirely on other family members to give their elderly relatives whatever care was needed while they were at work:

> Where [my husband] works, he works three days and has three days off and works three nights and has three nights off . . . I always work on a Wednesday and a Thursday. So [husband] either takes time off or a holiday period.
>
> (*Ms Rivers, part-time nursing auxiliary*)

For five carers, social services or hospital day care was an important source of substitute care, but as this did not entirely cover their working hours, they also relied on other family members to provide additional care for which they often made irregular or informal payments.

The remaining four carers all incurred regular and substantial expenditure on substitute care while they worked. Ms Dale's mother received day care four days a week in a private residential home at a weekly cost of £40 plus transport expenses. Ms Franks, who was a primary school head teacher, relied on a combination of social services day care and privately purchased domiciliary care:

> On two days a week the cleaning lady came in the morning . . . and it got to the stage where she could hardly do any cleaning for looking after my mother . . . the cleaning lady would leave about one o'clock and I'd try and get home at four o'clock. [Then one afternoon mother left the bath taps on and flooded the hall] so I got on to social services again and they found an extra day at the day centre . . . [and] another full day at an old people's home. So for three days we used to take my mother down to the day centre and collect her for four o'clock, which was very tying . . . on one day my cleaning lady condensed her [two half] days into one day and stayed with her – and *she* was neurotic at the end of it – and on the Friday my mother would go to the other old people's home.

For this substitute care, Ms Franks paid her 'cleaner' £15 a week; drove her mother to and from day care three times a week (no transport was provided); and paid £3.90 a week for her mother's lunches at the day centre. Ms Cox also paid her former 'cleaning lady'

£3 an hour to look after her mother while she herself worked full-time as a health visitor. Mr Dally employed an agency nurse at a cost of £180 a week to look after his mother while he worked full time in his pharmacy.

For some carers, then, the financial costs of retaining a full-time job while caring were considerable. However, they all had earnings which were high enough to bear these costs and they also had relatively high levels of seniority or autonomy. Other factors considered by the employed carers to be helpful included having understanding employers, flexible working arrangements – being able to take time off suddenly if an emergency arose at home for example – and the proximity of work and home:

> Being able to go flexible times. I could say 'I can't come in at 11, I can't come in till 12'. It wouldn't make any difference, that would be easy.
> (*Ms Harvester, about her part-time job as a living-out housekeeper*)

> It's with working locally that I'm alright . . . 'Cos some of them [other home helps] have to go to the next village. Well I couldn't do that, I'd be too long. But I know I'm here and I could soon get back to her.
> (*Ms Lincoln, employed part-time as a home help*)

Carers' commitment to paid work
Altogether, six of the 14 employed carers thought that the combination of employment and care-giving created considerable stress, although this was not yet serious enough to jeopardise their continuing employment or even lead them to consider finding another job, provided their relatives' care needs remained at their present levels.

Should those needs increase, however, around half of the employed carers thought they would probably stop work:

> The only thing is if [mother-in-law] becomes more disabled and has to be looked after, then obviously I would have to give up work . . . if she became bedridden . . . As I feel, if she got to such a state where she needed that care, I personally would think I would give it to her.
> (*Ms Anthony, employed part-time as an optician's receptionist*)

> If [mother]wasn't very well, I'd have to stop at home and look after her. I'd give my job up straight away.
> (*Ms Lincoln, working part-time as a home help*)

However, the other half were far more reluctant to consider giving up work. Significantly, this group contained almost all the carers working full-time, including the three full-time employed married women:

> I did consider a nursing home . . . which she wasn't happy to do . . . I was thinking in the future about the Cheshire Home or a private nursing home . . . and we put her name down to go into the Young Disabled Unit on a permanent basis as she deteriorated, but not until then . . . I like my job and I need my job and I don't see why I should have to give up – everything. Everything would have suffered, the family would have suffered . . . I just wasn't prepared to do it and I don't see why I should. I love my job.
> (*Ms McFee, full-time staff nurse in a mental handicap hospital*)

> I would have to have more help from the nursing side, coming in and bathing her, washing her . . . I enjoy me job . . . I can't do without working. I don't know how anybody would cope looking after someone all day every day. You can't do it.
> (*Ms Tree, part-time chain store supervisor*)

Of the carers currently in employment those working part-time or on a casual basis tended on the whole to be more prepared to consider giving up work altogether, should the disabled person's need for care increase. In contrast, those with full-time or long-established jobs seemed much less willing to consider making such a sacrifice.

These differences in carers' attachment to the labour market appeared to cut directly across conventional gender divisions. Both men and women, single and married, who had full-time professional or self-employed occupations which involved a career, responsibility or a long history as an economically active person, on the whole expressed a strong commitment to retaining this employment, regardless of possible increases in their relatives' care needs and in spite of the high levels of expenditure on substitute care. Carers in part-time work, on the other hand, were both less able financially to contemplate paying for substitute care and were also more willing to consider giving up their paid employment should more care be needed.

For the majority of these 14 employed carers, social security benefits offered no potential incentive to give up paid work in order to provide more care. Only Ms Halifax, working on a casual part-time basis for a clerical agency, said that she would stop altogether if she was certain of her eligibility for income replacement benefits. The remaining 13 carers, whether in full-time or part-time work, emphatically denied that social security provision might act as an incentive to stop work. These denials partly reflected a general lack of knowledge about potential benefit eligibility and partly an assumption that benefits would be far too low to be a viable alternative to even part-time work. However, more important than financial considerations were the psychological and social benefits which employment conferred, not just on the carer but indirectly on the disabled person as well. These benefits were stressed over and over again:

> I like my job, and providing I can carry on and get someone to look after [mother] I prefer it that way. It's not financial, [that] tends to balance itself out. It's psychological, I like it, I might feel lost not working.
> (*Mr Dally, a full-time self-employed pharmacist*)

> . . . it's also the fact that it gets me out . . . I can be absolutely shattered when I leave here at lunchtime, but the minute I walk in and get into the practice and those people come in, you're a different person. It's a therapy, so therefore it keeps me on an even keel. My working I think benefits everybody because I'm a much better person.
> (*Ms Anthony, part-time optician's receptionist*)

> I think it does us both good to be apart . . . to get away from her, having a fixed thing. And it gives her a degree of independence, a degree that she's needed [in order] to feel that *she* is needed.
> (*Ms Flaxman, casual relief nursery nurse at a special school*)

These carers were, in the main, already in employment at the time they had begun caring, and in various ways demonstrated their determination to continue doing do. To what extent did they differ from those who were already out of work when they began to care or who had since given up paid work?

Carers not currently in paid employment

The 16 carers who were currently not in paid work included four men, three of whom had specifically given up their last paid employment because of their mothers' needs for care. The 12 women not currently in employment were divided equally between those who were married and those who were currently single, widowed or divorced.

The married women who were not in employment tended to have left the labour market originally (though not necessarily recently) for reasons connected with child care. In contrast the men and the single women carers were more likely to have given up their last paid work because of care-giving, with unemployment and redundancy as subsidiary reasons for being out of work. However the distinction between these two groups was far from clear-cut. For example, a number of factors were sometimes involved in the decision to leave the labour market, of which the current or anticipated provision of care was only one. In addition some of the non-employed carers, both men and women, were still registering as available for paid work, even though they had very heavy caring commitments and would probably have found it extremely difficult to take up a paid job if offered one.

Out of work when care-giving began

Eight carers were not in paid employment at the time they began to provide a substantial amount of care, some because of redundancy or unemployment and some because of childbearing or other family reasons. None had therefore experienced any direct adverse effects on their employment as a consequence of caring. However, some did anticipate that their future employment prospects would be affected. Here the effects of age, gender and marital status in framing these prospects were clearly visible. Thus the younger single women and men all expressed firm intentions of becoming economically active in the future, although they recognised that the circumstances in which they could do so and the type of employment they might eventually be able to obtain would necessarily be limited. The married, older women on the other hand either definitely did not want any further paid work or else could not realistically envisage being able to obtain any, because of their age, lack of skills and length of time out of the labour market:

> I don't know. Sometimes I think I would [like a paid job again]. No, I don't honestly know what there would be now at my age and that, with no experience. There's not much around here . . .
> (Ms Carlisle, married, aged 52, made redundant from previous job)

> I don't want to work again. I'd be in the same position as what I was in before. Unless you're intelligent and got all your degrees at the back of you, I could only go out there and do what I was doing before, which . . . is labouring. And labouring wages are pathetic . . . If anything happens to me mother . . . and it's not all that far off really, I am expected to pick meself up, go back out there and start all over again. But the thing is, I was 36 when she [mother] came here; I'm now 47. Is there anyone who's going to employ me? I can't see it happening.
> (Ms Harris, widowed and unemployed before caring for her mother)

Giving up work to care

The remaining group of eight carers had all had some contact with the labour market around the time their relatives had begun to need a substantial amount of care. The provision of that care had led to a decision to stop paid work or not seek re-employment when their current employment ended. Mr Parks and Ms Bryan, both single, had given up part-time jobs – as manager of a menswear shop and a local authority clerk respectively – because of the increasing pressures on them at home. Mr Church, single, had given up his full-time job in a printing factory; and Ms Grey, married, had been a clerical assistant in a child welfare clinic but had also been forced to give this up soon after her mother came to live with her.

For two other carers, their respective mothers' increasing dependency had constituted a significant element along with other factors in the decision to stop paid work or not seek re-employment. The remaining carer, Mr Dawn, had been faced two years earlier with a choice between redundancy from his job as a French-polisher or taking an unskilled job instead. He had decided, with some relief, to opt for the former because of the increasing difficulty of leaving his mother on her own.

Most of these carers reported that their employment had already been affected before they had finally stopped work altogether. Three had switched from full- to part-time employment before giving up completely:

> Originally when me dad died I thought I'd have to finish work altogether . . . The first year I was trying to manage a shop and look after me mum. Well, that first year were sheer hell . . . In the end I had to have a word with one of the directors and tell them the situation. I'd been with the firm since I left school and they were very good and decided to give me this part-time job which would fit in with me home circumstances.
> (*Mr Parks, single, former menswear shop manager*)

Other carers had had to take extra time off or been interrupted at work by calls from home:

> I'd have to go home for hospital appointments because mother hadn't the intelligence to discuss with the doctor . . . I used to get a lot of rather annoying – to the firm they were annoying – 'phone calls from various people that used to ring up about her. It meant that I had to be broken off work, a security man would come for me, and I'd have to trail up to the telephone which would be quarter of an hour there and back.
> (*Mr Dawn, single, former French-polisher*)

Because of the impact of caring on their previous jobs, all of these carers had experienced reductions in their earnings prior to stopping work altogether:

> I was on piecework, which meant that my bonus was gone for the day [each time I was called to the 'phone].
> (*Mr Dawn*)

The most common reason for finally deciding to stop work altogether was the increasing amount of care which these carers were having to provide, and the difficulty this caused in also meeting the demands of a job:

> I just couldn't meet the requirements so I had to make the decision one way or the other then, it were either me mum or work.
> (*Mr Parks*)

Only three of the eight carers who had given up work had considered the possibility of making alternative arrangements such as buying in substitute care or arranging (more) day care provision for their respective parents, but all had concluded that this was not feasible:

> It was suggested by the housing manager, who was a lady, that I got someone to come in during the day to look after her. But I couldn't have coped because I wasn't getting any sleep. I couldn't have done both [work and care].
> (*Ms Bryan, single, previously working part-time as a local authority clerk*)

The extent to which these eight carers had considered in advance the financial consequences of stopping work very much reflected their gender and marital status. Two women who were married at the time of stopping work, and a third who was awaiting her divorce settlement, gave little thought to the financial implications. None had been in jobs where pension entitlements might be jeopardised by stopping work; for each of them it was only their current incomes which would be foregone. The husbands of the two married women were both in full-time employment at the time, and although the third anticipated being worse off, she knew she would be able to claim supplementary benefit as a separated woman.

In contrast, the five unmarried carers who had given up paid employment had been far more anxious about the financial consequences of this decision, and all had made systematic enquiries about their eligibility for benefits both in the short term and following their own eventual retirement. Mr Parks, for example, had sought detailed information from his local welfare rights advice service about unemployment and supplementary benefit, invalid care allowance and home responsibilities protection. Only when he was sure of his potential income from social security benefits and, eventually, from a frozen occupational pension, did he finally stop work:

> I were worried about the income more than anything, a regular weekly income.

Similarly Mr Dawn, faced with a choice between redundancy as a French-polisher and an unskilled job, had chosen the former only after having worked out exactly how he would manage financially:

> I weighed it all up and decided I could manage until I became of pensionable age. I'll receive the old age pension and a small pension from work which was frozen when I left . . .

When asked about their intentions of seeking employment again in the future, the age of these carers who had given up paid work seemed to be a key factor. Thus the older women and men either saw themselves as having left the labour market permanently or perceived their chances of future employment to be very slender:

> I wouldn't mind working at the day centre . . . So I've been to see – and they said they've cut down on their staff and they're relying on a lot of voluntary help now . . . I don't stand a chance now.
> (Ms Chester, aged 57)

Other, younger, carers hoped to be able to find paid work again in the future, although they recognised that they would be able to do this only on a very restricted basis while still caring.

Future prospects

Only a very small minority of the 16 carers who were currently not in paid work had any clear views about their future employment. Those who did tended to be older, married women who had already been out of the labour market at the time they began care-giving and who had neither the desire nor the financial pressure to become economically active once more. None of the other non-employed carers had any very firm intentions or plans. Most were aware that their current period out of the labour market would have an adverse effect on their future employment prospects and earnings, particularly when combined with other factors such as their advancing age and high local levels of unemployment. These carers were therefore aware that the future looked very uncertain, even after the period of care-giving was over. What had, initially, perhaps been thought of as a temporary withdrawal from the labour market might eventually turn out to be permanent retirement.

Conclusions

The effects of caring on the employment of these 30 carers were considerably varied. They indicate the many different circumstances which need to be taken into account in building up a comprehensive picture of the employment effects of care-giving and also warn against assuming a straightforward set of associations between gender, paid employment and unpaid care-giving. Certainly, the impact of gender can be detected in both the employment histories and the current labour market status of the carers. Thus, although there appeared to be no major difference between the men and women in terms of overall levels of economic activity, the female carers were much more likely than the male carers to be in part-time rather than full-time employment, both at the time they began providing care and currently. Men, on the other hand, appeared to be presented with a clearer choice between struggling to keep a full-time job and stopping paid work altogether. Even so this pattern was far from universal. Some married women were combining full-time paid work with caring (and had every intention of continuing to do so), while one man had negotiated a period of part-time work for himself before stopping work altogether.

The relationships between gender, paid employment and care-giving were, therefore, perhaps more complex than might have been anticipated. One unexpected pattern which emerged needs high-lighting. A very high proportion (11 out of 13) of the single, widowed or divorced carers who were currently living in a two-adult house-hold, alone with the person they were caring for, had either been out of work at the time they began giving care or had subsequently given up paid work to do so. In contrast, only a third of the carers who were living with another adult – a spouse or another unmarried sibling – as well as the disabled person were not economically active and only two had actually given up paid work to care. Almost two-thirds of the carers in these larger, three-adult households were, therefore, still in paid employment.

To some extent, this relationship between household composition and economic activity can be explained by gender and marital status: many of the carers in three-adult households were married women who, as has been suggested, were more likely to have part-time employment opportunities open to them. However, the three-adult households also included some single women carers who were living with unmarried brothers as well as the disabled or elderly person; and these women also seemed more likely to have retained their paid employment than those carers who were living alone with the disabled person.

The reasons for this association between marital status, household composition and economic activity can only be speculated upon. However, its *effects* – on the incomes of the carers and the living standards of their households – were substantial, as the next chapter will show.

Carers' incomes II: the impact of social security

This chapter will focus particularly on the extent to which social security benefits supplemented or replaced earnings which had been lost or foregone because of carers' responsibilities at home. Did social security benefits provide a level of income which meant that carers did not have to claim means-tested assistance benefits? Did carers have access to a level of income which did not entail dependency on the person being cared for? And did social security benefits encourage carers to give up employment in order to provide care? The first two of these issues have been highlighted because they featured prominently in the 1974 White Paper on social security provision for sick and disabled people (DHSS, 1974), in which an invalid care allowance (ICA) for carers who were unable to earn was first proposed:

> . . . the value of care in the family by the family when someone is willing to take responsibility is beyond dispute . . . There is a strong case for the provision of a non-contributory benefit as of right in these circumstances. (DHSS, 1974, p. 14)

The treatment of married women within these new social security arrangements was highly controversial (Finch and Groves, 1980; Finch and Groves, 1983). Originally assumed not to be members of the workforce ('they might be at home in any event', DHSS, 1974, p. 20), it was not until 1986 that their labour market participation was finally acknowledged and entitlement to ICA extended on the same grounds as other working age carers. In the following discussion it will be assumed that the personal incomes of married women carers need to be maintained in just the same way as other groups of carers, when they are partially or wholly prevented from earning an income from employment.

The study revealed some major differences in the social security entitlements, benefit receipt and personal and household income levels of those carers who were living alone with the person being cared for, and those who were living with one or more other working age adults as well as the disabled or elderly person. The former carers were single, widowed or divorced women and men. The latter group consisted mainly of married women and men living with a spouse (and sometimes young dependent or older, adult children as well), but also included a number of unmarried sisters and brothers who were still living together at home and, to a greater or lesser extent, sharing the care of a frail elderly parent.

The difference in income levels between these two types of household partly reflected the different patterns of carers' labour market partici- pation described at the end of the previous chapter. The extent to which social security provision modified or further accentuated those differences will be an additional theme in this chapter.

Two-adult households

Carers in employment

Only two of these two-adult household carers currently received earnings from employment: Mr Dally, a self-employed pharmacist, employed a private agency nurse to care for his mother while he was at work so that his income, estimated at between £14,000 and £18,000 a year, had been unaffected; and Ms Lincoln, who worked part-time as a home help. Her earnings of £35 (net) a week were nevertheless restricted by caring for her mother and were supplemented by widow's pensions of £44 a week. The earnings of both these carers were far too high to enable them to qualify for invalid care allowance, despite their high substitute care costs and restricted employment opportunities.

Carers without paid work

None of the remaining 11 carers living in two-adult households with the disabled person currently had any earnings from paid work. Despite considerable differences in their previous employment his- tories and the circumstances in which they had stopped work, this group of 11 non-employed carers now experienced very similar levels of impoverishment and financial insecurity. Their current income levels were apparently determined by a number of arbitrary and extraneous factors and without the cushioning of earnings from full- time employment, or a breadwinning spouse or sibling on whom they might depend, many were financially very vulnerable.

The social security benefits which these 11 carers received included invalid care allowance, supplementary benefit (at the then long- and short-term, householder and non-householder rates) and unemploy- ment benefit. Their main sources of income will be summarised, then the factors which determined their benefit eligibility will be discussed.

Only three of these 11 non-married, non-employed carers received invalid care allowance. All three had originally had to stop work because of care-giving. For two carers, ICA was their only source of income, as both were deemed to have savings over £3,000 which at that time rendered them ineligible for means-tested supplementary benefit. The third carer had her ICA topped up by the long-term rate of supplementary benefit, so ICA did not increase her overall level of income.

Two more carers received the long-term rate of supplementary benefit alone: one had not heard of ICA although she would almost certainly have qualified for it; the other was ineligible as her mother had been unsuccessful in applying for attendance allowance. Four more carers were signing on as available for work and therefore received only the lower short-term rate of supplementary benefit. For three of the four this was at the even lower non-householder rate, as their respective elderly parents were still officially the tenants or owners of their homes. Finally two carers, an unmarried woman and an unmarried man, relied on unemployment benefit, supplemented – and after a year replaced – by income derived from savings over £3,000.

Why were only three out of these 11 single, non-employed, full-time carers receiving invalid care allowance, the benefit intended specifically for them? The most common reason was that their relatives did not receive the attendance allowance. In only one instance had the relative actually applied but been unsuccessful; two carers had simply not heard of the attendance allowance; two disabled people had applied but not yet fulfilled the six-month waiting period (and one eventually died before doing so); and a sixth carer reported that his local DHSS office had told him that his mother would not be eligible because of the day care she received. The second most common reason for non-receipt of ICA was related to the level of the benefit. Because it was paid at such a low level, some carers knew that they would also be eligible for supplementary benefit, from which ICA would be offset in full:

> I realised that the supplementary were more than the invalid care allowance and I'd be worse off so I cancelled that. I wrote and said not to bother.
> (*Mr Teesdale, who received short-term, non-householder rate of supplementary benefit*)

Other carers had simply not heard of ICA, or were unclear about the eligibility criteria for the benefit:

I know, to get ICA, I do actually spend enough time with Jenny to get it; but do you think I could get that and not have to sign on? (*Ms Peel, currently receiving short-term rate supplementary benefit while caring for a friend*)

Some carers were unable to claim supplementary benefit because they were deemed to have savings over £3,000. Among these was Mr Parks, who had obtained Power of Attorney over his mother's affairs:

Me dad used to have a similar arrangement. There again of course when he died it was sorted out so that I'd be able to draw for her just the same. She couldn't really handle cash physically.

However, this power had been (incorrectly) regarded as giving *him* available capital over £3,000, despite the fact that he had virtually no savings of his own. Another of these carers, Mr Dawn, received neither supplementary benefit nor ICA. He had initially signed on and claimed unemployment benefit when he took redundancy in order to look after his mother. When his unemployment benefit ran out after a year, his savings rendered him ineligible for supplementary benefit; his mother's non-receipt of attendance allowance rendered him ineligible for ICA; and he lived entirely off the income from his savings.

Seven carers (five women and two men) were currently in receipt of supplementary benefit, three at the higher long-term rate because they had established that they did not need to be available for work and four at the short-term rate because they were still signing on as available for work. (Under the then supplementary benefit regulations, all four should have been exempt from the requirement to sign on and therefore eligible for the long-term rate.) By stating that they were available for work, these four carers were also unable to claim home responsibilities protection to safeguard their future retirement pensions.

Four of these seven supplementary benefit recipients were still living in their parents' homes and therefore received the even lower non-householder rate. In fact, one actually experienced an increase in his supplementary benefit when his mother eventually died, because he inherited her house and thus became entitled to the higher householder rate.

To summarise, these 13 unmarried carers in two-adult households had very different levels of income from a variety of social security and other sources. However, only two had incomes from paid work and in both instances these incomes had been reduced, indirectly or directly, by care-giving. None of the 11 non-employed carers had incomes above the long-term rate of supplementary benefit –

arguably, in view of their legitimate non-availability for work, an appropriate 'poverty line'. A number were living below that level.

These carers were also aware that their current financial situation was worryingly precarious. Their current income and benefit entitlements effectively depended entirely on their ability to continue giving care to a disabled or frail elderly person – someone whose own health and capacity to continue living at home could be highly problematic:

> I've got to think – if anything happened to me mother, say she were to pass away tonight – I've no job and nothing coming in at all, only perhaps interest from savings which wouldn't keep me . . . The only thing I worry about is if I lose my mother at this time of life, before I'm due for a pension – what's going to happen to me? . . . I'd have no income coming in as such and I'd be too old to get a job, quite frankly.
>
> (Ms Bryan, living on ICA plus £17 a week income from savings while caring for her mother)

Households with three or more adults

The low incomes and financial insecurity of the carers in two-adult households contrasted with the circumstances of the 17 who lived in larger households. The incomes of these three-adult households[1] were consistently higher than in the two-adult households. These differences were largely accounted for by the fact that *both* the carers *and* their partners or siblings were likely to have earnings from paid work. Two-thirds of the carers in these larger households had earnings of their own from full-time, part-time or casual employment, compared with only a sixth of the carers who were living in two-adult households.

Full-time employed carers

Five of the 17 carers (three women and two men) had earnings from full-time employment. Their current net incomes varied from £200 a week (Ms Franks, a primary school headteacher) to less than £70 earned by Mr Boot:

> I can't really put enough hours in . . . to earn enough money and ease the pressure of work . . . a bad week, it's next to nil, it just tapers off to an hour or two.
>
> (Mr Boot, self-employed auto-electric wholesaler)

---

[1] 'Three-adult household' refers throughout to those households with three or more adult members.

Altogether four of these five carers found their earnings reduced because of care-giving, or incurred regular and substantial costs in providing substitute care for their elderly relatives while they were out at work, thereby effectively reducing their disposable income. However, the hours and earnings limits on ICA meant that carers such as these were unable to qualify for any help to replace their lost or foregone earnings or to assist with their sometimes very high substitute care costs.

Nor did they see giving up work and claiming ICA instead as a realistic alternative to a full-time wage. Some carers also had doubts about their eligibility:

> ICA – I think it's £23 . . . That's what someone else said to me as well and I thought, 'There's a big difference from my wages'.
> (Ms McFee, employed full-time as a staff nurse)

> For a start I'd no intention of giving up work and I didn't think I'd qualify for supplementary benefit because my husband's income would have been too high. ICA – I didn't think that would apply because we had attendance allowance.
> (Ms Franks, primary school head teacher)

Part-time employees

A further six carers all had earnings from part-time or casual employment. Their current net earnings varied from £73 a week (Ms Tree, a chain store sales supervisor), to £15 a week (Ms Dale, who 'kept the books' at home for her husband's car-dealing business), to the irregular earnings of Ms Flaxman (a relief nursery nurse at a special school) and Ms Harvester (a cook/housekeeper and relief school cleaner). Like many of the full-time employees, most of these carers also reported that their earnings had been reduced or that additional opportunities to earn had been foregone since they began to provide a substantial amount of care.

Social security provision for carers in part-time employment is paradoxical and anomalous. These anomalies arise because of the ICA earnings limit and because of the problems of defining 'gainful employment'. Thus these carers were all in part-time jobs, and their employment opportunities and earnings restricted or reduced by the demands of caring. Although they tended not to have any direct extra expenses arising from the purchase of substitute care while they were at work (which could have been claimed as 'allowable work expenses'), such 'costs' nevertheless arose indirectly, through the carers' reduced availability for work and lowered earnings. As described in another recent study of live-in carers, 'their financial contribution took the form of the loss of their own earning power' (Horton and Berthoud, 1990, p. 33).

However, although the wages these carers earned were over the ICA earnings limit, they were often no higher than – and sometimes well below – the level of the benefit itself. The ICA earnings limit therefore effectively maintained their incomes at a level below that which would have been available through receipt of the benefit itself.

These carers' earnings were often well below the national insurance lower earnings limit as well, so they were also not paying national insurance contributions towards their own retirement pensions. At the same time their inability to claim ICA rendered them ineligible for the crediting of national insurance contributions, one of the automatic consequences of receiving the benefit.

Care-giving could, therefore, trap these part-time workers into very part-time, low-earning employment, in which both their incomes and national insurance cover were less adequate than they would have been had they been able to claim ICA. However, even though some of them would undoubtedly have been better off stopping paid work and claiming ICA, they saw little incentive to do so. Again, as with the full-time employed carers, they stressed the psychological and social, as well as the financial, benefits which paid work conferred.

Non-employed carers

Finally, there were six carers in the three-adult households, all married women, who had no incomes of their own at all. On the face of it, these six women appeared to be typical of the carers to benefit from the 1986 extension of ICA to married women. Did they know about the benefit at the time the interviews were carried out in the summer of 1986? Had they applied for it and what difference did they anticipate it would make if their application was successful?

Four of these six non-employed carers had already heard of ICA and three had already applied for the benefit in anticipation of its possible extension:

> I followed that case [Jackie Drake] on the news . . . My friend came over and said . . . 'Have you applied? Apply, you should get it' . . . We took me mum down to me brother's and his wife said 'Don't forget . . . make sure you apply for it'. So it was pressure from other people that I eventually did.
> (*Ms Johnson, unable to return to work when her mother developed Alzheimer's Disease and came to live with her*)

Having made the decision to care for their elderly relatives some time previously, the receipt of ICA would clearly not have any incentive effect. Instead, those carers who had already applied for the benefit anticipated that it would make a useful contribution to the house-keeping, helping to ease budgeting pressures and enabling extra 'treats' to be purchased – exactly the same uses, in effect, to which married women's secondary earnings from low paid or part-time employment are typically put (see Pahl, 1988):

> Maybe just to make things a bit easier – treats – for everybody concerned, outings. If we get a lump sum [arrears] I shall definitely consider having me bathroom altered, specifically with me mother in mind.
> (*Ms Johnson*)

However, a closer examination of the actual eligibility for ICA of these six non-employed married women revealed that only two would have benefited immediately from the extension of the benefit, and one of these had not yet heard of it. Of the others, Ms Lord was married to an unemployed man claiming supplementary benefit, so any ICA which she might receive would be offset in full against the benefit paid to her husband. Ms Grey had just passed her sixtieth birthday when she had to stop work to look after her mother and so was too old to receive ICA:

> I applied for this carer's allowance . . . because you're over 60 you're not entitled. I said – by the same ruling the European court said you could work while you were 65 and I was intending to, so why not [pay ICA till then]?

Ms Carlisle's mother had only just put in an application for attend-ance allowance, at least a year after she had probably first become eligible and until her mother was actually awarded the allowance, Ms Carlisle would be unable to claim ICA herself. Lastly, Ms Austin's mother had entered private residential care just before the extension of ICA was announced (though Ms Austin would probably have been eligible for arrears of ICA plus an extra-statutory payment from December 1984 until her mother's admission to residential care).

Discussion

Major changes in social security benefits have taken place since the interviews with these carers were carried out in 1986. Some of these changes will have had a direct impact on carers whose financial circumstances are similar to those described here. Most important has been the full extension of invalid care allowance to married women, resulting in an increase in the number of awards from around 5,000 in 1985 to 109,000 in 1988 (McLaughlin, 1991).

The 1986 Social Security Act also brought about some improvements for carers previously dependent on supplementary benefit. From 1988 the new income support scheme removed the different rates of benefit payable to 'long term', 'short term', 'householder' and 'non-householder' claimants. The savings limit below which income support could be claimed was raised from £3,000 to £6,000. However, the loss of the higher long-term rate of supplementary benefit was not compensated for by the introduction of a carer's income support premium (for ICA recipients only) until October 1990. Also in October 1990 the earnings limit for ICA was increased from £12 to £20, in April 1991 to £30 and from April 1992 to £40 a week (net of work expenses). The income support premium for ICA recipients has also been extended for eight weeks after care-giving ceases.

Despite these changes, a number of important issues are still highlighted by the findings of this study. The first is the low level of ICA, still only 60 per cent of contributory benefits and well below the single adult income support qualifying level. This differential has of course increased with the introduction of the new income support premium for carers, increasing yet further the difference between ICA and the means-tested income support minimum.

Secondly, even with the increased earnings limited, ICA recipients are still able to do only a minimal amount of paid work. The evidence from this study indicates that carers often want to continue working, even though they might actually be better off financially by not working and receiving ICA instead. The limited amount which ICA recipients can earn also means that there is no help at all for the majority of carers who remain in paid employment, who are nevertheless likely to experience reduced or foregone earnings or incur substantial substitute care costs in the course of working. Carers with very low earnings, just above the limit for ICA but below the national insurance lower earnings limit and even below the level of ICA itself, are particularly badly affected.

Thirdly, the linkage between ICA and the disabled person's receipt of attendance allowance effectively compromises the very principle of providing an independent income for carers. Carers in this study were providing substantial amounts of care for relatives who had nevertheless failed to qualify for the allowance; who had been misinformed about their potential eligibility; who had not heard of the allowance; who were currently waiting to fulfil the six-month qualifying period; or who, because of mental confusion, had failed to give an accurate account of their needs for help and supervision. This link between one person's benefit receipt and another's entitlement to an independent income, incorporating as it did difficulties in take-up and decision-making, had perhaps the single greatest impact on carers' social security entitlements and income levels.

Fourthly, there was no compensation at all for the earnings lost by carers who had continued to work beyond retirement age and then been forced to stop because of the demands of caring. Recent moves towards greater social security flexibility around the age of retirement (in particular the removal of the retirement condition and earnings rule affecting old-age pensions) make the rigid barring of older carers from benefits appear increasingly anomalous.

Finally, especially for those carers who had given up paid work altogether or who had seen a period of unemployment protracted by care-giving, there was considerable anxiety and uncertainty about the future. Immediately they ceased to give care (for whatever reason), their present benefit entitlements would cease and they would, if of working age, be expected to find employment again, regardless of the length of time they had been out of the labour market and regardless of the psychological and physical consequences of having been a carer. This insecurity has subsequently been exacerbated by the October 1988 decision that the national insurance credits received with ICA no longer count towards unemployment benefit which some carers might otherwise have claimed at the end of a period of intensive care-giving. The extension of the income support premium for eight weeks after care-giving ceases may help some carers through this difficult time, but its scope will inevitably be limited by the restrictions on both ICA and means-tested income support illustrated by this study.

Household incomes and other resources

This chapter describes some of the other financial resources available to the carers in the study and the ways in which carers maximised their incomes and living standards through the spending of savings, the increased use of credit or the accumulation of debts. These changes over time in the flows of household resources because of care-giving are important because they can reveal dimensions of financial hardship which might otherwise remain hidden.

Carers living alone with the person they were caring for naturally had only their own two incomes and savings on which to rely financially. As we have seen, both the carers and the disabled people in these households were likely to have very low incomes derived predominantly from social security benefits. Excluding the extra disability benefits – attendance allowance and mobility allowance – received by the disabled person, only very rarely did either the carers or those they helped have incomes which were above the notional 'poverty line' of 140 per cent of supplementary benefit entitlement. The majority had incomes well below that level.

In the remaining sixteen households, carers who lived with a spouse or another unmarried sibling as well as the disabled person had access to at least some of that person's financial resources as well. Moreover that adult was very likely to be contributing earnings from full- or part-time employment. Together with the carer's own earnings, this meant that half of these 16 households had one full-time and one part-time wage coming in, and nearly a quarter had two full-time wages or salaries. In principle, therefore, these additional household (as opposed to individual) resources could make a substantial difference to the household's overall standard of living.

Moreover, because this group of carers generally shared their households with another employed adult, the impact of any adverse effects on their *own* employment and earnings may have been cushioned. Was there any evidence that the incomes of these other household members – particularly those who were in full-time employment – compensated for the loss or reduction in the carers' own incomes?

Incomes of additional household members

Both the form in which other household members contributed to the household budget and the levels of those contributions varied considerably. On the one hand a married carer like Mr Boot, looking after his father, had access to all his wife's income through the 'pooled' system of housekeeping (Pahl, 1989) which they operated together. On the other hand a single carer like Ms Tree, living with her unmarried brother and caring for their frail elderly mother, bought all their weekly shopping from her own earned income while relying on her brother to pay the major household bills out of his earnings.

The incomes of the other members of the three-adult households varied considerably, from the manual wages of Ms Carlisle's brother (a brewery tanker driver's mate), the non-manual earnings of Ms Cox and Ms Grey's husbands (retail trade managers), to the professional salaries of Ms Austin's husband (an export sales manager) and Ms Franks' husband (a chartered surveyor). However, almost a third of these other household members were reported to have experienced some adverse effects on their own employment since the period of intensive care-giving began. For example, Ms Anthony's husband had changed to a less demanding and stressful job since his mother had come to live with them. Ms Tree's brother, a self-employed clog-maker, now had to leave work at 3.30 p.m. each day, to relieve a second sister who sat with their mother while Ms Tree herself was at work. Mr Boot's wife similarly found her hours of work and earnings reduced:

> She's self-employed, freelance design work. It just slows her down a bit. There's all things like the laundry – there's a lot of work up till dinner time, she's got to wash the bedclothes every day.

Ms Johnson's husband worked as a lorry driver:

> I sleep in, I can't get up. [My husband's] always been a right good time-keeper but . . . They'll dock him [wages] this week because he's been late for work and that's been my fault because I've been up in the night with me mum.

Moreover none of these full-time employed partners or siblings was reported to have *increased* their own earnings to compensate for the reduction or loss of the carer's income to the household. The financial 'protection' offered by other earners in the household was therefore very limited; not only were they unable to compensate for the loss of the carer's earnings, but their own incomes were likely to have suffered as well.

Savings, credit and debt

Despite the considerable differences between the carers in the two- and three-adult households in both their individual and household incomes, their levels of savings and the incidence of credit and debt showed some surprising similarities. However, there were differences between the two types of household in the ways these savings were used, and in the overall incidence of greater financial hardship.

Availability and use of savings

Fewer than half of the 13 carers living in two-adult households had any significant additional financial resources of their own. Only five stated that they had savings of more than £3,000. Four of these five carers were currently making substantial use of these savings, particularly the interest which they generated. Mr Dally, a self-employed pharmacist, drew on them to help meet the high costs of substitute care for his mother while he was at work, Mr Dawn lived entirely off his savings and Ms Bryan and Ms Halifax used the income from their savings to supplement their only other income, from ICA and unemployment benefit respectively:

> I'll pay an instalment off me rates and draw some out, because I think if I've got more than £3,000 I won't get anything [supplementary benefit] anyway, so I just keep using a little bit.
> (Ms Halifax)

The remaining eight carers in two-adult households had very few savings:

> I did have savings, a small amount, but I spent it on me correspondence course when I gave up work . . . I've about three insurance policies, I'm using them as me savings now.
> (Mr Parks, who received only invalid care allowance)

The seventeen carers living in three-adult households appeared to be no more likely than those in two-adult households to have substantial savings they could fall back on. Eight had savings over £3,000, although several said that these were only 'just above' the £3,000 mark. However what did differentiate these households from the two-person households was the frequency with which savings were drawn on to supplement other sources of household income, and the uses to which they were put. They were not, as in the two-adult households, drawn on regularly to meet essential or basic household expenditure such as fuel and rates bills or house repairs, but to pay for holidays, new furnishings, or extra items which were needed because of care-giving or disability. Such expenditure was particularly likely to have occurred when a disabled person first moved to live in the carer's household:

> We have drawn out quite a bit. We'd to buy a bed for mum to come here . . . You're talking about £150 for a bed . . . one or two little draw-outs like that.
> (*Ms Grey, married woman who stopped her part-time job after her mother came to live with her*)

> A couple of bits of savings I had put away, I had to use for her when she first came because she didn't have any supplementary benefit or anything because her books had to go back, so she came and she'd absolutely nothing, no clothes and no money. So this is where my expense came in, drawing out of me bank account to keep her going till her money came through. The back-pay [supplementary benefit arrears] went into *her* bank account.
> (*Ms McFee, married woman working full-time whose mother was discharged from hospital after a major operation to live with her*)

Changes in budgeting strategies

Care-giving also had longer-term financial consequences. If resources were attenuated over an extended period of time, then different strategies of managing money had to be adopted in order to maximise carers' current income, albeit at the expense of their longer-term financial security. These strategies included changes in the use of loans and credit, changes in the ability to put aside savings and meet bills on time and changes in patterns of consumption, whereby some types of expenditure were reduced or foregone so that others could be afforded.

Almost all of the two-adult household carers had had to employ longer-term economising strategies as a consequence of care-giving. One carer had had to buy more goods on credit, one often delayed paying bills and two said they had cashed insurance policies as they could no longer afford the premiums. One carer had had to borrow money because she was unable to earn, and five said they were no longer able to save for the future:

> If I was still working full-time, I'd think nothing of putting money away.
> (*Ms Halifax, unmarried woman claiming unemployment benefit and drawing on her savings*)

> Yes, it has affected my savings, because if I'd have had a full-time job I'd put so much away. I'd normally have done that.
> (*Ms Chester, unmarried woman who received supplementary benefit at the long-term rate*)

Five of these carers also said that they had cut down on personal spending because of the drop in their income levels since becoming full-time carers:

> I go out less for drinks, less visiting friends, going to listen to music. I smoke less – I'm desperately trying to give up smoking.
> (*Ms Peel, single woman caring for her friend, who received short-term rate supplementary benefit*)

> I used to go out for a drink now and again. Well I don't do that any more. I can't get out and I haven't the money to do it. Smoking – I'm packing that up and all, that's too dear. My social life, you can say I've cut down on that.
> (*Ms Harris, widowed and receiving long-term rate supplementary benefit*)

In the three-adult households, seven of the 17 carers had also adopted additional strategies to make ends meet because of care-giving; delaying paying bills, foregoing consumer items they would otherwise have bought, not saving as much as they would have done and borrowing money:

> We've always spent our money on enabling the boys to do . . . we've tried to compensate them a bit because they missed out on things like holidays and having as free a life as they would possibly have had . . . We didn't have a car . . . We only had a scooter because at that time we couldn't afford to do the things we did *and* have a car as well.
> (*Ms Rivers, married woman working part-time and looking after her father-in-law*)

However, there was a contrast with the carers in the two-adult households. As with their use of savings, the borrowing and economising in these three-adult households was not so much the result of day-to-day financial pressures, but because of the specific extra items needed by the disabled person. For example, Ms Johnson and her husband had had to take out a loan to buy a car before they had finished saving up for it, in order to prevent the whole family becoming housebound:

> We had a van which we were thinking of changing to a car. Within three weeks of me mother coming, we went out and bought a car simply because we couldn't go out otherwise as a family because we couldn't get me mother in the van . . . We had to have a car there and then because we were more or less housebound that Christmas.

Mr and Ms Anthony had taken out a loan and second mortgage to build an extension to their house to accommodate Mr Anthony's mother:

> We took it out for £5,000 and they put 60 per cent of it on the mortgage but we had to pay back the extra £2,000 over 5 years on a loan . . . At the time it was a hard time.

Finally, about a third of the carers, divided equally between the two types of household, admitted to increased anxiety about their financial circumstances or anticipated a change in circumstances which would increase their financial insecurity within the foreseeable future. These heightened anxieties were prompted by the prospect of the carer's or the disabled person's savings running out or by the carer's own imminent retirement from work:

> If she [mother] spent that capital . . . somehow you'd feel wide open, you feel a bit vulnerable. With having that capital, it's just something at the back of you all the time. If something goes wrong, you've always that money at the back of you.
> (*Mr Parks, single man, who received only ICA*)

> I don't worry yet, but I could do. I don't mind for another year or so, but then I'll tend to think about things more seriously [when I retire myself].
> (*Mr Dally, full-time self-employed as a pharmacist and paying substantial amounts of money on substitute care for his mother*)

> As we get older and we go onto a pension, if she's still at home when we're pensioners, I think it will be more difficult then.
> (*Ms Flaxman, casually employed as a supply teacher, caring for her adult daughter*)

Conclusions

Although there was less evidence of immediate financial strain, the evidence of longer-term financial pressures was almost as widespread among the three-adult households as among the carers who lived alone with people they cared for. However, both the causes and the patterns of these pressures appeared to be different. It seemed that in the three-adult households they were less the result of day-to-day hardship and poverty, but resulted instead from extra spending on disability or care-related items. This extra spending was also more likely to have been of a one-off kind, and to have arisen early on, at the time when joint care-giving households had been formed. The carers in two-person households, on the other hand, having generally never left their parental homes, had no such costs arising from joint household formation; but their lower household and personal incomes created considerable day-to-day financial strains. Both types of household also appeared equally vulnerable to financial anxieties in the future, as savings became depleted or carers approaching retirement anticipated a substantial reduction in their own incomes.

Nevertheless, the resources entering the three-adult households were clearly much higher than in the smaller households. This was not just because these carers lived with a spouse or sibling who often had earnings from full-time work. It was also because the carers themselves were more likely to have paid employment – albeit with levels of earnings which were lower than they would otherwise have been. Neither they nor their households therefore experienced the more acute hardship and insecurity characteristic of some of the carers who lived alone with the person they were looking after.

The extra costs of disability and care-giving

Although there is a substantial body of detailed evidence on the extra expenses incurred by disabled people (see Martin and White, 1988; Smyth and Robus, 1989; DSS, 1990b; DIG, 1988, 1990), less attention has been paid to the extra expenditure incurred as a result of giving help, support and personal care. The most detailed evidence on the costs of care-giving is in relation to disabled children (see Bradshaw, 1980; Glendinning, 1983; Baldwin, 1985). Studies of the care of disabled or frail elderly adults have been less systematic in their examination of the extra costs of care-giving. The majority of Nissel and Bonnerjea's (1983, p. 49) 14 owner-occupier carers had incurred additional expenditure on moving or altering their homes. Many also complained of heavy additional spending on heating, laundry, linen and special foods which was not covered by the elderly person's income. However Nissel and Bonnerjea did not apparently investigate exactly what income and savings the frail elderly people had, which of these resources were actually contributed to the household expenditure, nor what other longer-term or non-material resources might be contributed by the elderly person and others to offset these extra costs. The information collected by Levin et al. (1989, p. 119) was restricted to extra expenditure incurred by the supporters of confused elderly people during the preceding month, but again extra heating bills and laundry costs were prominent.

The distinction between the costs which arise because of the special needs of a disabled person and costs which are incurred because of, or in the course of, giving care is not always easy. For example, ramps, handrails and special bathroom fittings may be considered as costs arising from disability; simply building an extra room onto the house to accommodate an additional household member who needs help may be construed as a cost of care-giving. In other instances the distinction may be far less clear. For example, although an automatic washing machine may be needed because of the incontinence of a disabled person, it also undoubtedly helps a carer in coping with the extra laundry which results.

However, whether certain costs are to be classified as disability or care-related may not matter very much if, at the end of the day, they both fall on the carer. It is important, therefore, to identify contributions which the disabled person, other relatives and statutory agencies make towards any extra expenses. The distinction is also important in considering the policy implications of carers' extra spending, because any such extra costs could either be recompensed by an increase in the incomes of disabled people (or those elements in their incomes which are intended to provide for the extra costs of disabled living), or by directing additional financial help towards carers.

One-off 'capital' costs

Housing alterations

Just over half the households had made some kind of alteration to their homes to accommodate the disabled person or make it easier to look after her/him. However, these alterations were usually not very extensive and their entire cost had rarely been borne solely by the carer (and her/his family). This was partly because few of the disabled people suffered exclusively from physical and locomotor impairments, and partly because those who did tended, in the course of hospital-based rehabilitation, to have been put in touch with local authority services for adapting and equipping accommodation for disabled people.

The most common alterations were the installation of ramps and handrails and showers specially for use by the disabled person. Other households had installed new bathrooms and/or toilets, usually downstairs, or built (or were currently planning) an extra downstairs room to become the disabled person's bedroom. More minor alterations included additional locks and safety gates, paving the area outside the house to make it wheelchair-accessible, installing extra handrails inside the house, altering or moving doorways, installing bath hoists and moving door handles.

Many of these alterations had been carried out together as part of a 'package', with particularly extensive 'packages' having been carried out by five households. Each of the disabled people in these households had severe physical disabilities and had initially received extensive hospital treatment and rehabilitation. As they had neared discharge, it had become clear that they would need adapted accommodation:

> We've got a ramp and rails. We had the back garden – my husband's terraced it and concreted it for her . . . The doors are all

sliding, downstairs. She's got her own bath and rails by the toilet. She's got pull switches over her bed and electric switches . . . that she can reach from her bed . . . the bathroom and toilet downstairs was built for her and we had the extension built, the extra bedroom. What is her bathroom used to be the kitchen, so we had *this* kitchen built on and we had this room partitioned.

(*Ms Flaxman, married woman looking after her daughter who had been disabled by a viral inflammation of the spine at the age of 16*)

We had an extra wide step put on the back so that she could actually get in and out of the house; a couple of extra rails here and there for when she goes in the loo to help her get down and up again . . . Her room [added on to the side of the house] was tailor-made. We've had all the plugs put high up with on and off switches, we bought special plugs with the handles . . .

(*Ms Anthony, married woman whose mother-in-law moved to live with her after treatment in hospital for severe osteo- and rheumatoid arthritis*)

The adaptations carried out in the remaining households consisted mainly of installing items like showers, handrails or extra locks to prevent a confused elderly person from wandering:

We put a shower in so she didn't need to sit down in the bath. We did move door handles – we took them off so she couldn't rattle them. If there was a door locked she'd rattle them so much she broke one or two of them.

(*Ms Franks, married woman, whose mother had senile dementia*)

So far as the cost of these adaptations were concerned, in a third of the 15 households no extra costs fell on the carers or their families, because the disabled person, another relative or statutory sources had covered the entire cost:

We didn't have to pay anything [for Helen's purpose-built bedroom and bathroom extension]. There's a special fund where adaptations for disabled people – and they were prepared to pay half the extension that we wanted, to correspond with disabled accommodation, the recommended space for a wheelchair user . . . Anyway just as they passed it as OK, they brought in that we could get an improvement grant . . . so therefore with the two grants put together that paid for all the alterations.

(*Ms Flaxman*)

In another six instances the cost to the carer (and her/his family) was relatively small – extra locks, do-it-yourself garden paving and shower fittings. None was reported to have caused any debts or financial difficulties. However, in four households substantial expenses had been, or were about to be, incurred by carers. Ms Rivers had installed a downstairs toilet and washbasin and extended their kitchen when her father-in-law came to live with them. Even with an improvement grant and a contribution from the sale of Mr Rivers senior's house, the extension had still, in 1970, cost them an additional £2,000 which they had paid for by extending their mort-gage. Following her mother's stroke, Ms Dale and her family had sold their house and moved into her mother's house. There they had built a new bathroom, toilet, shower and downstairs bedroom; and installed a ramp, extra paving and widened doorways. The bathroom fittings had been paid for by a small grant from the social services department and the remainder – between £10,000 and £12,000 – by Mr and Ms Dale themselves. Ms McFee's planned ground floor extension (to provide a separate bedroom for her mother who was currently sharing with a teenage granddaughter) was expected to cost her and her husband £8,000. Both Ms McFee and Ms Anthony (who had also built a ground floor extension and installed external ramp and rails to accommodate her mother-in-law) considered that these adaptations had caused considerable financial stress. Although Ms Anthony had enquired about the possibility of statutory help towards this adaptation, she had not been able to obtain it:

> I went to the CAB, I didn't go to social services. I said 'Would we get any help?' and she said 'No not really, because it's part of *your* property' . . . I really think they could have provided or given us help towards a shower because we were doing everything else ourselves.

However, some of this major capital expense had been offset by the £20 a week 'rent' which Ms Anthony's mother-in-law gave to them:

> This is how in the very beginning she came to pay rent, purely to pay that bank loan off, because we couldn't have met that bank loan without her money, on what *we* were earning.

In summary, many of the housing adaptations and minor alterations which carers had paid for had arisen because of the specialised needs of the disabled person. However, there was no guarantee that these costs would be borne either by the disabled person or by the statutory services. The chances of some contribution towards the cost through social services departments, housing departments or improvement grants seemed highest when the disabled person had previously experienced a period of in-patient hospital treatment. Discharge arrangements might then include information and advice about appropriate accommodation.

However, the majority of the people being cared for in this study had had no such period of hospitalisation when any special needs for housing adaptations might have been identified. Some had simply remained living in their own homes as their needs for care had increased. Others had moved to live with sons and daughters without the involvement of any professionals at all. Here, alterations were not necessarily required because of any specialised needs the disabled person had, but simply because an additional person had come to live in the household. Furthermore, where alterations had been carried out to the carer's rather than the disabled person's home, carers may have been more likely to see their financing as *their* responsibility rather than that of the disabled person or the statutory services. Even when alterations were extensive, the fact that it was the carer's home to which adaptations were being carried out could still make it difficult to secure financial help, as Ms Anthony's experience showed.

Consumer durables

Here the distinction between disability and care-related expenditure is much harder to sustain. Virtually all the 29 households had acquired at least one major item of household equipment or consumer durable. Many, such as laundry appliances, helped directly to ease the extra work involved in care giving. Others, such as dishwashers and freezers, saved carers' time and effort in other areas of domestic work. Extra television sets, radios and videos, however, might be thought of as more for the direct benefit of a housebound disabled person, although they could hardly be considered as specialist disability aids.

Not only is the disability/care-giving distinction harder to maintain here, but many consumer durables might also benefit all the members of the care-giving household. If such items would not have been acquired but for the presence of the disabled person, then their purchase could perhaps be construed as leading to a higher standard of living for carers and their families than would otherwise have been the case. In this context, the question of who paid for and who benefited from any such acquisitions becomes crucially important.

The most common consumer durables which were acquired were an extra television set for the disabled person's bedroom, washing machines and tumble driers. Other households had bought a video, dishwasher, liquidiser, deep freezer and extra radio.

In only one instance had financial help towards this extra household equipment come from outside the household; Ms Peel's own parents had bought a washing machine and food processor for her and her friend Jenny. In four more instances the cost of additional consumer durables had been met wholly from the disabled person's resources. For example, Ms Grey's mother had brought her own television with her when she moved to live with Ms Grey and her husband and continued to pay the rental on it from her own income; Ms Frank's mother had bought a video when she came to live with her. A few large household items were bought jointly by the carer and disabled person: Ms Peel and Jenny had just bought a fridge-freezer for £180; Ms Bell and her mother had split the cost of a £250 washing machine, as had Mr Teesdale and his mother.

In all these instances, there was likely to have been some net gain for the carers, who were benefiting to some extent from the acquisition of a major consumer durable to which they had contributed no more than half of the purchase price.

This left a total of 13 carers – nearly half the sample – who had themselves (and their spouses) paid for one or more additional consumer durable during the previous five years, at costs ranging from £50 (for a second-hand colour television which Mr Teesdale had bought for his mother), to an estimated total of £500 rental which Ms Rivers and her husband had paid on an extra television for Mr Rivers senior. The average extra expenditure by these 13 carers was £227.30. In only two instances did carers consider that they had had difficulty paying for or contributing towards these extra items. Ms Peel, herself dependent on short-term supplementary benefit, had had a struggle to find £90 towards their jointly-purchased fridge-freezer, while Ms McFee had spent £240 on an extra television and clock radio:

> Mother wanted a colour one [for her bedroom]. I said I couldn't afford to do that, so she said if I got it in my name, she would pay me, pay it off. Well she didn't do . . . It's another £11 a month that I'm paying that wasn't necessary, and she wouldn't pay it.

Special aids and equipment

Virtually all of the 29 households had acquired at least one piece of specialised equipment or aid for their disabled relative, most commonly commodes or chemical toilets, wheelchairs, special tables or trays designed for use in an armchair or bed, walking frames, sticks or other mobility aids, and special armchairs, bedding, cushions or sheepskins. There was a clear pattern whereby younger disabled people or those with predominantly physical impairments had acquired a much larger number of special aids than those who were generally old and frail.

The majority of these specialised aids had been obtained free of charge from the local social services department or the district health authority's community nursing service. Others had been lent or purchased by relatives or friends.

Of the remainder, about half had been paid for by the disabled person her/himself; and half by the carer (and her/his spouse). On the whole, the aids paid for by carers tended to be smaller, non-specialised items, such as trays and tables to fit over armchairs and beds, costing £35 on average. Stairgates, intercoms and walking frames which had been purchased privately were equally inexpensive. Two carers had bought high armchairs for their elderly relatives. These two carers had also spent by far the largest total sums of money on special aids for their respective mothers:

> The commode, we bought it, it's a chemical toilet. I bought a chair, an upright for her room. I bought her a special mattress when she had the stroke. I bought that . . . it was thicker than normal. And I bought a tray for over the bed.
> (*Ms Robbins, non-employed married woman*)

One other type of equipment which a number of carers had acquired because of care-giving was a telephone or special telephone-linked facilities. A total of 12 carers had acquired one or more such items. In the main this had meant installing a telephone for the first time or an extra telephone extension socket which would not otherwise have been needed. In addition, Ms Peel's friend Jenny and Mr Parks' mother both had telephones linked to other electronically-operated equipment.

Only one of these telephone installations had been paid for entirely by the carer, and in two other instances the cost had been split between the disabled person and carer. Nevertheless, two of these three carers had found it difficult to afford their financial contribution towards the telephone installation:

> I played hell actually. It were me brothers that demanded it [the telephone] . . . but they didn't give me anything towards it.
> (*Mr Teesdale, unmarried man looking after his disabled mother*)

Again, therefore, it was clear that some carers could find themselves paying towards equipment and aids which were needed primarily because of their relatives' disabilities. While social services departments and community nursing services were likely to help with larger and more specialised items, and help from other relatives was also sometimes forthcoming, carers themselves were still likely to have purchased a range of smaller, non-specialist aids and equipment. In a few instances, total spending on several of these smaller items could be quite substantial.

In summary, most of the carers had experienced at least one type of extra expenditure on adaptations, aids, consumer durables or special equipment in the relatively recent past. Some of this was related to the work of care-giving or to the general accommodation of an additional household member, as well as to specific disability needs. The incidence of such expenditure did not appear to be restricted to carers who had relatively high levels of household income; carers who were not in paid work had also saved money from weekly social security benefits or drawn on their savings to pay for extra items. There were a few instances in which carers had incurred very substantial extra expenditure which they considered had resulted in some financial hardship and stress.

Recurrent extra household expenditure

Both disability and care-giving can also incur recurrent extra spending on items needed because of disability (extra warmth, special food, extra laundry and toiletries needed because of incontinence, for example); and on labour-saving and time-saving items to ease the work of care-giving (buying 'convenience' foods and ready-made clothing, for example, instead of making one's own).

Heating and other fuel costs

The most common source of extra expense was on heating and other forms of fuel consumption.

A third of the 29 households had had extra heating installed or had purchased additional heating appliances specifically because of the disabled person, including the installation of full central heating:

> Well we had the central heating in . . . because at the time, as I say, if she wasn't well we used to take electric fires or convector heaters [into her bedroom]. So we thought we might as well go in for [central] heating.
> (*Ms Lord, married woman, whose mother was frail and partially sighted*)

Three more households had changed to safer forms of heating, usually from solid fuel open fires to gas fires:

> We did have an open fire when mother came here. It was a new one and we decided to get rid of it because we'd had one or two loose coals. At that time she was staggering and I didn't want anything to happen to her . . . and then she got lost looking for coal. So then we went in for gas fires.
> (*Ms Grey, married woman, whose mother had senile dementia*)

Another three carers had bought extra electric or calor gas fires, mainly for heating the disabled person's bedroom in winter, and Ms Dale had installed additional radiators in the extension she and her husband had had built, which had also involved installing a new central heating boiler.

In most instances, the cost of these heating installations had been borne entirely by the carers. The sums which fell on carers ranged from £35 (for an extra electric fire purchased a year ago by Mr Church for his elderly mother), to the £1500 it had cost Ms Flaxman and her husband to install central heating eight years earlier for their daughter Helen. The average for each carer was around £400.

Paying for these extra heating installations had not been without difficulties. For example, Mr and Ms Flaxman had had to take out a second mortgage to pay for their central heating system and Ms Lord's central heating had been paid for with a five year loan. Her husband's unemployment two years later had created great difficulties in meeting the repayments.

Although only a third of the sample had bought or installed extra heating appliances, four-fifths considered that their recurrent fuel bills were higher because of the disabled person. The most common reasons for this were that central heating or other heating appliances were now kept on all day, that the room where the disabled person usually sat during the day needed to be heated to a higher temperature, that extra hot water and electricity were needed for the additional laundry generated by the disabled person, or that the disabled person's bedroom needed to be heated at night, particularly in winter:

> We had to have the heating on all day, every day . . . She used to sit in the lounge and it's the biggest room in the house and it's impossible to keep warm – she was always cold . . . It's normally on twice a day but when me mother was here it was on constantly in winter – you couldn't possibly switch it off.
> (*Ms Austin, non-employed married woman*)

> When it's cold we keep the [central] heating on quite a long time into the night . . . In the depths of winter it's on more or less 24 hours a day.
> (*Ms Tree, part-time employed single woman caring for her mother*)

While most carers had little difficulty in identifying the reasons why they spent extra on heating and fuel, they found it much harder to estimate the proportion of the total fuel bill which could be attributed to the disabled person's need for *extra* fuel. Estimates of extra fuel consumption were more easily arrived at where the disabled person had recently joined the household, died or entered residential care:

> You see, the quarter before, when mother was at [my sister's], it was £160, so [last quarter] was £104 more . . . Since we've got mother we've been averaging somewhere around £300 a quarter, whereas we used to keep it down to £160 . . . it's just about £100 a quarter more. That's gas and electricity together.
> (*Ms Robbins, married woman looking after her physically frail elderly mother*)

Of the carers who were able to make an estimate, about half thought that their previous fuel bills had more or less doubled:

> Astronomical that was . . . It actually doubled our heating bill . . . it was about £120 more than it was the previous year for that quarter.
> (*Ms Austin, married woman whose mother had senile dementia*)

Mr Dally estimated that 75 per cent of his annual fuel expenditure resulted from his mother's need for extra heating (her room had to be heated day and night) and extra laundry. Ms McFee and Ms Bryan thought they spent 50 per cent more; Ms Robbins estimated an extra 40 per cent; and Ms Chester, Ms Franks and Mr Boot all estimated that their fuel bills had been increased by around a third.

Despite these sometimes enormous increases in carers' fuel bills, only three carers admitted to difficulty in paying them. Some economised wherever they could by running the washing machine on an Economy 7 meter, doing washing by hand and switching off the central heating system whenever possible. For a second group, budget accounts and pre-payment meters helped in managing high expenditure:

> Before I had me [central] heating put in [because of mother] I had a meter . . . They advised me to go onto quarterly bills which I did do because of the heating, they said it was more convenient . . . But then they became too excessive when [husband] finished work, so I went on the – like paying for it monthly, like on a budget scheme. But . . . it comes that I couldn't pay the bills . . . so they came and asked me would I mind if they put a meter back in for me, and I didn't . . . Now it's £1 coins.
> (*Ms Lord, married to an unemployed man, and looking after her frail, partially sighted mother*)

A third group used part of the disabled person's resources – attendance allowance, occupational pension or savings – as a form of short-term saving, keeping them to one side and drawing on them when fuel bills were due:

Electric I pay from mother's [bank] account too – gas, electric and rates I have done.
(*Mr Dally, unmarried man looking after his frail elderly mother*)

Food and laundry

Far fewer carers reported extra spending on food, over and above what they would have expected to spend for a household of that size. Only one carer said that his mother had to follow a special diet, the cost of which was not offset by savings on ordinary food:

> She gets a lot of health foods that are more expensive usually; and she's got to be on fibre-rich foods, wholefoods, which are usually more expensive than the refined variety . . . So far as meat's concerned, you daren't get meat with a lot of fat on . . . 'cos she has difficulty with chewing . . . and getting it digested.
> (*Mr Parks, single man caring for his mother*)

Just under half the sample reported that they bought treats or special kinds of food for their disabled relatives, either to tempt her/his appetite or because s/he preferred to eat different things from the rest of the family. Even so, extra spending on special food or treats such as these was again frequently offset by reduced spending on other food items. Only two carers were able clearly to identify net extra expenditure which arose in this way:

> My brother spends an awful lot on fruit, because she sits and eats fruit all day.
> (*Ms Carlisle, married woman whose mother had dementia*)

> Two pounds of sugar would do us. Now, I can use six pounds a week. You're talking about three teaspoons of sugar in every cup of tea . . . she can go through two pounds of syrup a week. She must have lost her taste buds, but they say this is part of the dementia. And salt . . . cakes, and anything with cream.
> (*Ms Grey, married woman caring for her mother*)

Six of the 29 carers also cited extra spending because their disabled relatives had capricious appetites or destroyed food:

> Half past three, four o'clock time . . . she thinks that me dad's coming home, it's teatime, and she goes back to when she looked after all her brothers and all the men'd be coming home; and she gets a loaf of bread and butters a full loaf of bread . . . We do waste an awful lot of food of every kind because [my brother] . . . cooks, gets all the best meat and vegetables and she just goes round everything and mixing it all and touching it all and wrapping it in filthy things. We waste an awful lot of food.
> (*Ms Carlisle, married woman whose mother suffered from dementia*)

A fourth cause of extra spending on food was the purchase of more expensive food, either because carers had less time to shop around or do their own baking or because they bought ready-made or take-away meals as a treat to compensate for some of the other restrictions on their lives:

> For convenience I go to Marks and Spencers. When I had time, I would bake and make a lot of my own stuff. I just don't have time in the mornings now, because she does take up time.
> (*Ms Anthony, married woman who looked after her mother-in-law*)

> It's very rarely I go down the market now – mostly I go to Sainsbury's . . . You tend to treat yourself more, have nice things to eat more. I definitely spend more on food.
> (*Ms Peel, unmarried woman caring for a disabled friend*)

Even though these carers were largely responsible for budgeting and shopping for food, they were still not easily able to estimate how much extra was spend on food, over and above what would be expected for a household of that size. In addition a number of carers were aware that they spent more on the cared-for person's food than was strictly necessary, because this constituted an expression of affection and care. This emotional component to food purchase made some carers very unwilling to attach monetary values to their extra expenditure:

> I might subsidise her a little with odd treats.
> (*Ms Anthony*)

However, despite these difficulties, just under half the sample considered they spent more on food than they would expect to for a household of their size.

About three-quarters of the sample considered that they had extra washing and drying over and above what would be expected for a household of that size. This was most often caused by incontinence and clumsiness:

> She used to have her bed changed every single day. Sometimes you'd have to change it in the middle of the night as well if she'd decided to take her knickers off . . . Sometimes you'd have to clean her up completely from top to bottom during the day.
> (*Ms Austin, married woman whose mother had senile dementia*)

The 21 carers who had extra laundry reported an average of just over three *extra* loads of washing each week. Six carers estimated only one extra load each while, at the other end of the spectrum, Ms Austin had seven because of her mother's incontinence and clumsiness; and Ms Johnson did eight, for similar reasons:

> I had got down to washing on a Monday and a Thursday for the children . . . but now I wash bedding every day, and an extra load of clothing every two days.
> (*Ms Johnson, married woman, whose mother had dementia*)

Two carers also spent extra on dry cleaning. In Ms Cox's case, it was her *own* clothes which needed cleaning after being soiled by her mother's incontinence. Ms Frank's mother, on the other hand, soiled two or three coats every fortnight, incurring an estimated £150 a year extra on dry cleaning bills. The incidence of extra spending on dry cleaning was however lower than might have been expected because most carers deliberately avoided buying clothing and furniture coverings which were not washable:

> I don't [spend extra on dry cleaning] simply because I buy things that wash. I overlook tags that say 'To be dry cleaned'.
> (*Ms Johnson*)

This widespread practice may, on the other hand, have pushed up the extra expenditure on laundry.

The actual levels of extra spending on laundry and dry cleaning by the carers in this study depended on the type of appliances used and, in particular, whether expensive tumble driers were used instead of cheaper methods of drying clothes and bedding. Assuming the cost of fuel and detergent for one load of washing to be 50 pence, the 21 carers who could specify how much extra washing and dry cleaning they had to do spent an average of £1.80 extra each week (£93.60 a year), plus any extra fuel costs for drying clothes.

Extra clothing and bedding

Incontinence and extra laundry are among the commonest reasons for needing extra clothing and/or bedding. About half the carers said their relatives needed extra clothing and footwear:

> She needed a new pair of slippers about every three weeks because she'd messed them up. I'd just throw them away.
> (*Ms Austin, married woman whose mother had senile dementia*)

> Clothes – like trousers and that – it's ridiculous. Not that they wear out more quickly, but you have to wash them more so you need more to circulate.
> (*Ms Peel, single woman whose friend Jenny had a severe spinal injury*)

Some carers had bought special clothes which were easier to get on and off:

> I've . . . had to buy her things that were easier to put on . . . it's been things in a stretchy material that will go over her arms, and a button-through that I could do up rather than having to go over her head.
> (*Ms Cox, married woman whose mother had senile dementia*)

Other reasons for needing extra clothing, though less common, could nevertheless be costly:

> She's put on an awful lot of weight since she's come to live here, which I put down to the [increased] sugar intake. We've had to buy quite a number of new clothes. I've had new pinafore dresses made for her. She was a size 10 when she came here, she's now in a 14 to 16.
> (*Ms Grey, married woman whose mother had senile dementia*)

> When she came she'd no clothes at all because she was in hospital for three months and all her clothes [at home] were damp and ruined. When she came [here] from hospital she had a dressing gown, a nightdress, a tracksuit bottom, one vest, toothbrush . . . she hadn't a skirt, a jumper . . . She came on the Friday night and I went out and spent £150 on the Saturday.
> (*Ms McFee*)

Not all these extra clothing needs fell exclusively on carers. In only four of the 14 instances in which the disabled person needed extra clothing were all of these purchased entirely by the carer:

> It's come out of mine [money]. I've bought whatever she's needed and I haven't bought it out of her money.
> (*Ms Cox*)

In half the households in which extra clothing needs arose, the cost was shared between the carer and either the disabled person or other relatives:

> Me and me sister between us [have bought new clothes] . . . Two pinafore dresses that came last week, they cost £22, £11 each. [My sister] has bought her two pinafore dresses . . . I've bought three pinnies for her and my sister's bought some for her.
> (*Ms Grey, married woman whose mother had dementia*)

In these latter situations, carers and other relatives often used Christmas and birthdays as occasions for providing clothing.

Two carers also reported extra wear and tear on their own clothing, Ms Flaxman from lifting her daughter Helen's wheelchair in and out of the car and Ms Austin because of her mother's incontinence. However, neither felt that this resulted in noticeable extra expense. Two other carers spent more on their own clothing because they no longer had the time to hunt for bargains or to make their own clothes. In contrast, some carers considered that they now spent less on their own clothes than previously, either because they had far fewer opportunities to go out socially or because giving up work meant they needed fewer smart clothes:

> I don't get out that much so I aren't really that bothered about buying clothes . . . I spend less because I don't have time to actually look around and I don't see things that I would see if I had time. And not having a lot of time to go anywhere, I don't need the clothes.
> (*Ms Tree, single woman caring for her frail elderly mother*)

To the extent that these economies reflected a reduction in the levels of consumption by carers and a lowering of their standards of living, such 'savings' could be construed as additional 'costs' for carers.

About half of the carers needed extra bedding, almost invariably because of incontinence. However, disposable sheets from the health authority could help, and elderly relatives who had given up their own homes to come and live with carers sometimes brought ample stocks of bedding with them; tearing up old sheets to use as drawsheets could also help to reduce extra bedding costs:

> I didn't buy any extra bedding because my friend, her mum went into a nursing home and I got all her bedding and I just cut that up.
> (*Ms Austin, married woman whose mother had dementia*)

As a result of such strategies, only a few of the carers who needed extra bedding had actually spent extra money on this during the preceding year. Where this did occur, it was almost invariably paid for by the carer alone and the average extra cost was quite high – £61.50 over the previous twelve months – mainly because it included not only bed linen, but also washable duvets, pillows and mattresses.

Household cleaning and repairs
Toiletries and cleaning materials, especially related to incontinence, were a very common cause of extra spending, reported by over three-quarters of carers. The majority spent over £1 a week extra, five carers were each spending at least £4 a week extra and one was spending over £6 a week on talcum, toilet rolls, cotton wool, chemicals for the

chemical toilet in her mother's bedroom, air fresheners and soap powder:

> I had eight toilet rolls a week and she'd go through those like nobody's business . . . I went through a lot of Dettol, air fresheners and soap powder. Soap powder's 86 pence a box – I was using two boxes a week. Tissues are 48 pence – about two [a week] . . . A couple of bottles of Dettol a week . . . I used to get a big air freshener, then those blocks every week.
> (*Ms Austin, married woman whose mother had senile dementia*)

Invariably the cost of these extra cleaning items and toiletries was met by carers out of the weekly housekeeping.

Three-quarters of carers also reported extra damage or wear and tear around the house. Most commonly this was because of incontinence which caused damage to floorcoverings and furniture, or wheelchairs and walking frames which wore down carpets and chipped paint-work. A less common cause was clumsiness or aggressiveness which resulted in ornaments and crockery being broken, food being spilt, or lighted cigarettes being dropped on chairs and bedding:

> The easy chair she sits in . . . because when you lift her into it, sometimes you nearly drop her into it if you don't lift her right and it puts a lot of weight on the back; we usually find the backs go first.
> (*Mr Parks, whose mother had multiple sclerosis*)

> He drops things. We've lost the handles off cups and beakers, anything that he touches, general crockery . . . He's so unsteady when he walks that if anything happens to be near the edge, off it goes.
> (*Ms Rivers*)

Despite the prevalence of such wear and tear, very few carers reported actually having spent extra money on replacements or repairs during the previous year. Some items had not been replaced, either because they were not essential (such as broken ornaments) or because they were still serviceable (Ms Franks, for example, had not replaced the tables and sideboard whose tops had been damaged by dripping water when her mother had let the bath overflow). Some carers who had given up paid work now spent less on redecoration and repairs because they were able to do more themselves instead of having to pay someone else.

Consequently only a third of the carers who reported extra household damage also reported recent extra spending. This ranged from a few pounds on extra paint to 'touch up' wheelchair-damaged walls and woodwork, or a new rug to replace one damaged by spilt food, through an average annual expenditure of £40–£50 on replacing broken crockery, to major one-off items such as a new three piece suite at £300 or new carpets and furniture. In almost all these instances it was the carer who met these extra costs.

Staying in touch: transport and telephones

Half of the carers reported regularly using their telephone more, because frequent contact with medical, nursing or social services was needed, because carers were in regular contact with other relatives about the disabled person's health or care, or because the disabled people themselves regularly made long-distance telephone calls to other relatives and friends for which the carer paid:

> We do use it more to inform me brother, especially if she [mother] is not well or she's gone into hospital.
> (*Ms Lord, married woman whose mother was frail and partially blind*)

Half the carers who reported extra use of their telephones also said that the bills were sometimes higher than they expected or that they had on occasions experienced difficulty paying them. Ms Khan, for example, was under constant threat of having her telephone cut off and often had to borrow money to avert this. Carers bought telephone stamps each week or set up monthly budget payments to prevent such crises occurring, but this was still not always successful:

> I had one [bill] in particular for £125 which was quite a shock . . . I pay it in a budget account through the bank anyway, so my payments monthly went up sky high for that bill.
> (*Ms McFee*)

On the whole, responsibility for paying the telephone bills lay with carers (and their spouses), out of their own income(s). The only exceptions were two households in which carers and disabled people made roughly equal contributions to the purchase of telephone stamps, regardless of their respective usage.

Over half of the 29 households owned a private car. Four carers said that they had had to buy a car or an extra car which they would otherwise have managed without, and three said that they had had to buy a larger car than they would otherwise have needed.

Nine car owners said that they regularly used their vehicles more than normal, for general social activities for the disabled person, because of the carer's shortage of time, or to provide transport to hospital, respite care or day care:

[I use the car more] to take her out; and also she does have day care, so to take her there and pick her up again. And to go to the shops, which sounds ridiculous; but when you've only got 20 minutes [if] she's here on her own, even the shops round the corner here, if I walk . . . I'm out over half an hour.

(*Ms Dale, married woman whose mother had had a major stroke*)

Other extra transport expenses were identified by nearly half the carers, sometimes on top of the expense of running a car. These included hiring taxis for the disabled person or carer, paying friends or relatives for providing lifts and, in the case of Mr Parks, an additional £30 a year RAC membership because of the risk of breaking down when out in the car with his mother.

Altogether, just over half the carers identified one or more source of regular extra spending on transport. However, by no means all of these extra costs fell on carers themselves:

We've got a jar for the car. Whereas I put in money for petrol, she puts in the whole mobility allowance for repairs or anything else that needs doing for the car . . . With [me] going to college . . . I tend to put a bit more in for petrol. It makes my life much more convenient being able to get to college quicker in the morning and being able to get home quicker in the evening.

(*Ms Peel, looking after her friend Jenny who had a spinal injury*)

However, the entire burden of extra transport costs – whether buying a (bigger) car, using it more often, hiring taxis or paying others for lifts – did fall exclusively on over a quarter of the carers. For example, Ms Lord estimated that taxi fares for her mother to visit relatives and for herself to get home quickly from shopping amounted to about £90 a year, while Ms Dale estimated that, on top of the cost of purchasing a larger car, she spent well over £1,000 a year extra on petrol.

Five of the people receiving care received the mobility allowance. However, this did not necessarily cover all their carers' extra transport costs. Moreover a number of other carers incurred extra expenses, either in providing transport for the disabled person or in using more expensive but more convenient forms of transport themselves, for which no social security benefits were received. Nor were these extra transport costs fully offset by the other money which the disabled person contributed to the housekeeping and general household expenses.

Deferred and foregone expenditure

The amounts which carers actually spent in caring for their disabled and elderly relatives were constrained in two important respects.

First, carers and disabled people who have only very low incomes are likely to report levels of extra expenditure which are markedly lower than those incurred by more affluent households, simply because they cannot afford to spend as much (Baldwin, 1985; Martin and White, 1988; DSS, 1990b). Among lower income households, therefore, actual expenditure may fall short of the items or commodities which are needed.

This was certainly true of a number of these households. Around a fifth of carers identified disability or care-related needs which they were simply unable to afford. Most of these were major household items – floorcoverings and furnishings – which had been badly damaged, especially by incontinence or the rubbing of wheelchairs. Because carers were unable to afford to replace them, they had to continue using worn or soiled items or just manage without:

> [Before my mother came] we'd just got me daughter's bedroom done up, got her a pink carpet. You can imagine when I was toileting mother, sometimes she was wetting on the floor . . . Can't afford to replace the carpet just yet.
> (*Ms McFee, married woman, whose mother had to share her daughter's bedroom*)

> Yes, I had to throw two carpets away upstairs . . . she soiled them completely. I tried and scrubbed. I've not been able to replace them yet.
> (*Mr Teesdale, unmarried man looking after his mother*)

Two carers, living on very low levels of social security benefits, indicated unmet needs for even more basic items such as warm clothes and housing repairs. Because of the combination of their very low incomes and the extra costs of caring for a disabled person, they were simply unable to afford these. Ms Khan, for instance, aged 19 and looking after her disabled mother, was unable to afford to replace the carpets, beds and bedding which had been damaged by incontinence and she and her mother now slept downstairs on settees. She was unable to afford to keep their very damp house as warm as her mother needed, and also to buy her mother a coat, despite her mother's poor mobility and chest problems. Ms Harris too had housing repair problems:

> I'd like to have a brand new wall at the back. I'd like that hole mended behind me kitchen sink. I would like floorboards under me bath.
> (*Ms Harris, widow, caring for her elderly mother*)

A second group of carers, around a sixth of the study sample, were explicitly postponing some types of extra expenditure until the period of care-giving was over. Again this was particularly true when floorcoverings, furnishings and bedding had been worn or damaged. Ms Austin's mother, who had dementia and cancer, had just entered a residential care home, and this had prompted a major financial outlay replacing and repairing furnishings which had been damaged:

> The carpets – the toilet carpet has been completely replaced, and the bathroom carpet; and the bedroom carpet I just ripped out because it was absolutely – yuk . . . She wouldn't bother where she put her hand when she was trying to clean herself up, so everything had to be decorated. You cleaned and cleaned until you couldn't clean it . . . the walls were covered where she had been. We had the lounge decorated . . . and her bedroom was refurnished completely.

For some carers, questions referring only to current or recent spending may result in serious underestimates of total extra expenditure. First, they may overlook sometimes substantial spending which is being deferred until the period of care-giving is over. Secondly, a significant minority of carers may be unable to afford some of the extra items needed by the person they are caring for or, because of spending on such items, may be unable to afford other items which might be regarded as household or personal necessities.

Disability or caring costs?

It is clear that a number of common items of extra expenditure incurred by carers arose directly from the special needs of the disabled person. Specialised housing adaptations, extra heating, additional laundry, clothing, bedding and toiletries all resulted from disability rather than care-giving. The fact that some or all of these costs could be met by the carer resulted partly from the inadequacy of the disabled person's financial resources and partly from the systems of household financial management which carers and disabled people had negotiated between them (see Chapter 9).

There were also a number of instances in which carers incurred extra expenditure by virtue of their care-giving role – expenditure which, moreover, was not offset by the resources contributed by the disabled person nor compensated for by reduced spending in other areas. Although not all the carers in this study experienced all of the different sources of extra spending of this kind, most did experience at least one and in some instances this extra spending could be substantial.

Some of the most substantial sums of money spent by carers specifically because of care-giving were on substitute care – particularly when this had to be comprehensive and reliable enough to enable carers to retain full-time employment. Other substantial sums were sometimes spent by carers whose disabled relatives had given up their own homes and moved into the carer's household. Apart from specialised disability-related alterations, carers also often made other changes to their homes simply in order to accommodate an additional person without undue inconvenience to her/him or the rest of the household.

A third cluster of items which constituted care-related costs reflected the restrictions which carers now felt on the time available for domestic and household work. In different ways they paid for others to do some of this work instead. They bought more expensive convenience foods or no longer had time to shop around. Extra money was spent on transport for similar reasons – carers drove or took taxis to the shops because they could not be out for long. Decorating and dressmaking were other services which carers effectively had to buy in because they no longer had time to do their own.

Fourthly, there was a miscellaneous group of care-related items such as cleaning and replacing carers' own clothes which were soiled or disproportionately worn, telephone charges to keep in touch with other relatives about the health of the disabled person and fares and other expenses when visiting the disabled person in hospital.

It is difficult to quantify these exclusively care-related costs, in part because their incidence among this small sample was so variable. There is no doubt, however, that for some carers these costs were considerable. Far more widespread were costs associated with disability which also fell upon carers, despite the disability benefits which the disabled people received and the financial contributions which they made towards the general household expenditure.

Patterns of responsibility and control over household financial management

This chapter examines how the two separate economic units of the disabled person and carer interacted within a common household structure.

It is concerned essentially with issues of control. Where did control over the carer's and the disabled person's resources lie? Who decided what resources should be available for items of collective household consumption? Who took decisions about budgeting on a day-to-day basis to ensure that collectively-consumed goods and services were paid for? Who was responsible for deciding on major, one-off items such as redecoration or new furniture?

The issue of control is distinct from the more practical one of who physically handled money within the household. It is also analytically distinct from that of the actual *amounts* of money which were made available by the disabled person and carer (and other family members) towards items of joint household consumption.

Allocating and pooling different types of income

Research on patterns of money management within marriage has shown a clear tendency in low income families for all household resources to be pooled and managed by one person (Pahl, 1989); and among this sample of carers the members of the poorest households were indeed likely to make more of their own personal financial resources available to a common 'pool' for collective expenditure, than were the members of more comfortably-off households. Ms Lord, a carer whose husband had recently become unemployed, described this shift towards a greater pooling of household resources as their financial situation had deteriorated:

> [Now] she [mother] gets her money and we pay out of ours what we can pay out; and then her money is there and it's more or less

put together . . . [Before] it was just left there – I used to draw her money for her and we used to do out of ours what we had; we used to do our shopping and put the bills away and everything. Basically her money was *her* money . . . But now, it's used every week for whatever . . . it varies. From week to week you can budget, but when you get the 'phone bill in – this one is £50-odd and it'll take all his money to pay that and I haven't got a penny so that week I'll have virtually nothing so I've got to draw on mother's money.

A subsidiary dimension of the patterns of money management within these care-giving households was the specific uses to which particular types of income or benefit were put. Thus the basic income mainten-ance benefits received by the cared-for person (retirement pension, supplementary pension, invalidity benefit or severe disablement allowance) were usually put towards the weekly shopping and other bills which were paid on a weekly basis. Disability benefits – attendance allowance and mobility allowance – tended to be saved towards more intermittent bills (especially telephone and fuel bills), if the total household income was high enough to afford this degree of short-term saving. In the poorest households the attendance allowance was pooled along with all other available income to provide the greatest possible flexibility in budgeting. On the other hand, occupational pensions and savings held by the disabled person were more likely to be reserved for major items of personal expenditure – clothing, aids, or holidays – or simply accumulated as long-term savings.

In almost all the households the main carer (and occasionally her/his spouse) was primarily responsible for all the weekly household budgeting and shopping – food, cleaning items, toiletries, etc. The disabled people were slightly more likely to take some responsibility for the payment of regular larger bills, such as rent, rates, gas, electricity and telephone. In addition, in six of the households the disabled person was jointly or solely responsible for decisions about big, one-off items of expenditure like redecorating or buying new furniture.

Nevertheless, control over financial affairs even in these latter house-holds still rested predominantly with the carers. In no instance did the disabled person exercise control over any part of her/his carer's income or other resources. Rather, it was the carers (plus spouses) who, as 'housekeepers', had access to and command over some or all of the resources of those they were caring for.

Patterns of control

Within this overall framework, three main patterns of financial responsibility and control involving disabled people and carers could be detected.

Carer control

In the most common pattern the carer was responsible for all the household budgeting *and* had effective control over all the disabled persons' financial resources. The carer would draw the disabled persons' social security benefits and any occupational pension, and would also have access to any of her/his savings. The carer then allocated these resources towards different areas of household and care-related expenditure as s/he thought appropriate. In some households this arrangement had been formalised through the carer being the signatory on social security order books or obtaining Power of Attorney over her/his relative's financial affairs:

> At one time he used to pay us so much of his own volition and then he got so he didn't really know what he were doing. We were finding pound notes stuffed down the back of radiators, that sort of thing. The Post Office suggested – I hadn't realised that I could actually sign his name.
>
> (*Mr Boot, married man, who cared for his father*)

This pattern of complete carer control was most likely to occur when the disabled person was now living in the household of the carer (and spouse); and, in particular, when s/he was suffering from a substantial degree of mental confusion.

Even though the carer had access to all the disabled person's money, this did not necessarily mean that all of this money was pooled or added to a common housekeeping 'kitty'. Different benefits were allocated to different items of expenditure (for example, the attendance allowance might be saved towards fuel bills while the retirement pension went into the weekly housekeeping) and unallocated money was sometimes saved in the disabled person's bank account. The important point here is that *decisions* about this allocation were taken entirely by the carer:

> [My brother cashes her pension and] he brings the money home and it goes towards paying grocery bills, milk bills, things like that. The rest of it goes away for larger bills, the gas, the rates.
>
> (*Ms Tree, unmarried woman who lived with an unmarried brother and their confused elderly mother*)

A variant of this pattern was for a small proportion of the disabled person's money to be returned as 'pocket money':

I cash her pension, give her some spending money, £10, then I put
£10 in the building society and pay the milk fortnightly and the
papers out of it and anything that's left goes into the building
society.
(Ms Halifax, unmarried woman caring for her mother)

Occasionally the sum which was handed back as 'pocket money' was
large enough to enable the disabled person to save towards clothes,
holidays and presents for grandchildren. More often, especially
among elderly relatives who were suffering from dementia, this
personal spending money had a token significance only.

Whatever the amount of 'pocket money' returned to the disabled
person, and whatever actual or symbolic items of personal expenditure it was intended to cover, the important point is that its size was
determined entirely by the carer in exactly the same way as s/he
allocated the rest of the disabled person's income between food, fuel
bills and other items of household expenditure.

Joint control

Here the disabled person exercised a substantially greater degree of
control over her/his own income and other resources. This control
might include the retention of a sizeable sum of personal spending
money. Alternatively the disabled person might allocate all her/his
resources towards the collective housekeeping pool. The significant
feature however was the degree of involvement in, or control over,
this decision.

The retention of this degree of control was clearly associated with an
absence of mental confusion on the part of the disabled person; the
disabled people who operated this pattern all had physical rather
than mental disabilities.

Within this category were two sub-groups, depending on whether
the carer or the disabled person had a history of responsibility for the
expenditure of that household. In the first sub-group the disabled
person had moved to live with the carer after the onset of her/his need
for care. Here the disabled person decided on and gave her/his
contribution to the carer, who then took complete responsibility for
managing their joint household budget and expenditure, including
the payment of housing costs. For example, Ms Anthony's mother-
in-law had come to live with her, her husband and their two teenage
daughters after developing severe rheumatoid and osteo-arthritis.
She decided how to allocate her income, but assigned to Ms and Mr
Anthony responsibility for the household budgeting:

We [mother-in-law and I] do the 'phone bill between us. The girls
have a little bit of spends [from her]; then she puts her club money
away, her insurance money; then she puts the money away for her
TV rental because she pays that; then money to me for food; money
to [husband] for her rent; and then the rest is hers . . . It's her
independence, it's her money.

In the second sub-group the disabled person was not only involved in
decisions about how much money she or he should contribute to the
common housekeeping pool, but also retained some responsibility
for the management of that money. This tended to occur where the
disabled person had historically been the householder in what was
now a shared household, or where the carer and disabled person
explicitly held joint householder status. For example, Ms Halifax and
Mr Parks both still lived at home in their parents' household. Their
respective mothers retained control over their own money, deciding
in consultation with their carers how much to allocate to the collective
household expenditure. Both parents were also involved in decisions
about exactly how that money was spent, particularly when it came to
major items of expenditure such as furniture, redecorating and
housing repairs:

If there's a repair needs doing and we need the money out of the
bank, then I suggest it to me mum and she says whether we can go
ahead and get it done.
(*Mr Parks, unmarried man, whose mother had multiple sclerosis*)

Separate areas of control

Here the disabled person and carer each retained some degree of
control over their own incomes and also had entirely separate areas of
responsibility for at least some specified items of household spending. For example, Mr Church and his 69 year-old mother operated
this system in a relatively 'pure' form, with no pooling whatsoever of
individual incomes. Mrs Church was the householder (Mr Church
had returned to live with her following his divorce) and was still
responsible for their joint housing costs:

I pay for all the groceries and she pays the rent, and I buy a few
other things she might want, like cigarettes. The big bills, we share
those.

In the other two households in this group, this 'separate areas of
responsibility' pattern operated in a modified form, in which individual control over personal incomes and separate responsibilities for
specified areas of household spending operated alongside a greater or
lesser degree of pooling of resources.

The factors which seemed to be associated with this pattern were somewhat less clear than the previous two systems of financial control. The one factor which was clearly important was the disabled person's status as the householder of the dwelling which she now shared with the carer; this was reflected in the fact that the areas of household expenditure which the disabled person was responsible for meeting from her/his own income tended to be associated with housing costs (rent, rates and repairs) or major household assets.

Explaining patterns of household financial management

In summary, there appeared to be three main patterns determining the degrees of control which carers and disabled people exercised over their own incomes and over the management of the household's finances. These appeared to result from the intersection of two separate dimensions: the degree of control which the disabled person exercised over her/his own financial resources; and the degree of involvement and control which s/he exercised over the management of common household expenditure and consumption.

Affecting these dimensions were two important factors. One was whether the disabled person or the carer had a history of responsibility for household budgeting in the dwelling in which they now lived together. The disabled person's householder status was enhanced where it also coincided with a parent/child kin relationship with the carer – that is, where the carer was an unmarried son or daughter who had never left home or had returned to live with an elderly parent following divorce or widowhood. Conversely, in those households in which the carer (married or unmarried) had lived before the arrival of the disabled person, the carer was far more likely to have complete control over the household's financial management.

The second factor was the degree of incapacity, particularly mental incapacity, of the disabled person. Indeed it seemed that the presence of mental confusion was a primary determinant of whether the disabled person had any control over her own income or any involvement in the management of collective household expenditure. Where mental confusion did not exist, the disabled person's householder status then determined the particular areas of collective expenditure over which s/he exercised any control.

Although there was some evidence of a relationship between total household income and patterns of household financial management, this relationship was far from consistent and was complicated by differences in householder status and the type of disability involved.

Conflicts over financial issues

The incidence of conflicts between carers and disabled people is important, because social and fiscal policies tend to be formulated around assumptions about single income unit households and not, as was common among this group of carers, households containing more than one income and tax 'unit'. Moreover both the formal benefit entitlements and actual living standards of both care-givers and disabled people were substantially interdependent. To what extent did carers or disabled people experience difficulties or disadvantage at each other's expense?

Conflicts of interest between carers and disabled people were less widespread than might perhaps have been expected and there were few instances in which any such difficulties actually resulted in adverse financial effects on carers. In only about a fifth of the households did carers report any difficulty at all in obtaining access to sufficient levels of resources from the people they were looking after and in only one instance had these difficulties resulted in actual financial disadvantage for the carer. Undoubtedly this reflected the mental confusion of many of the disabled people, who may have had little understanding of the financial management being carried out on their behalf:

> She's probably a bit in pocket, but having said that, mum doesn't *feel* that she's in pocket, because she doesn't control her own money. It's a war every Tuesday, I hate Tuesdays. Because she'll say 'Is that all I have left?' and I'll say 'But mum, there's lighting and heating and everything' . . . I find it very difficult, the money part. She's been very independent, that's the thing, she won't let go.
> (*Ms Grey, married woman, whose mother had Alzheimer's disease. Ms Grey cashed and kept her mother's attendance allowance each week and gave her mother her pension but asked for £25 of it back as a 'board and lodging' payment*)

Nevertheless, some carers expressed reluctance at exercising this degree of control, which appeared to stem from a feeling that, as sons and daughters, they were violating a norm of parental authority by exercising control over their parents' money. However, the alternative to exercising such scruples would have been financial disadvantage for both themselves and the disabled person, and this provided a powerful incentive for carers to overcome their reluctance:

> The consultant at [the] hospital advised me to take Power of Attorney and do it quick while she was aware and able to agree. I didn't want to . . . feel that I was responsible for her money.
> (*Ms Cox, married woman, caring for her mother*)

The only household in which the disabled person's financial contribution was a source of conflict and had cost implications for the carer
was Ms McFee's. Ms McFee had initially spent a considerable amount
of money buying clothes, a television set and radio for which she had
not been reimbursed. Disagreements about Ms McFee's mother's
contributions towards expenditure on her behalf continued to charac-
terise their relationship, and may have contributed to its eventual
breakdown:

> The £20 [a week contribution to the housekeeping] was her
> suggestion . . . I wasn't happy about it when I discovered I had
> extra expenses, but that was all she was prepared to give. You can't
> get blood out of a stone. It was her money after all.

The overall financial impact of caring

Measuring the overall financial impact

This chapter examines the incomes and other resources which the carers and disabled people had available to them and the uses to which those resources were put. Against these resources are placed the various demands which had to be satisfied: everyday housekeeping and daily living costs; extra costs arising from disability and infirmity; and the additional expenditure incurred in the course of care-giving. The assessment also considers some of the longer term dimensions of expenditure patterns, resource management and resource transfers between individual household members. These include spending which was delayed or deferred, and past or future transfers of resources to the carer which might help to offset any current lost earnings or extra spending.

This assessment takes into account more than simple changes in overall levels of household expenditure. It also includes changes in the types and quality of the commodities and services consumed by the various household members – in particular, changes in consumption by one household member at the expense of the standard of living and quality of life of others. For example, although total expenditure may remain the same, spending may be switched from one type of commodity to another, with the *benefits* of that expenditure transferred from one household member to another. Similarly, a reduction in total household income because of lost earnings may be absorbed by one person making substantial changes to her/his own patterns of personal consumption in order to protect the other members of the household from a deterioration in their living standards. To the extent that such changes in intra-household patterns of consumption involve a reduction in the material quality of life of the carer, they should properly be considered as part of the costs incurred by carers.

In order to assess the overall financial impact of caring, a 'balance sheet' for each household was constructed. It was assumed that economies of scale would take place through the sharing of some commodities and housing costs, and that these economies would be similar for all the households. Apart from these, the 'balance sheet' assessed whether the resources contributed by the cared-for person actually covered her/his regular daily living costs – the cost simply of having an additional person in the household – and the extra expenses which arose because of disability. To what extent did these remain outstanding, to be met in effect from the resources of the carer?

The assessment also included one-off, capital and deferred items of expenditure and longer term transfers of resources between disabled people and carers – savings, loans and purchases of major consumer items from which both benefited.

All this information was assembled for each household in the study and used to form an overall assessment of the extent and nature of the financial impact of care-giving on each of them. It also revealed some differences in the kinds of financial effects experienced by different types of households.

Regular patterns of spending

Across the sample as a whole, carers combining full-time employment with substantial amounts of care-giving were likely to experience high levels of spending on substitute care. Therefore, although these carers may have managed to avoid some of the longer term costs of caring – downward occupational mobility and reduced rates of pay – typically associated with interrupted employment or periods of part-time work (Joshi, 1987), the impact on their disposable incomes in the short term could nevertheless be considerable.

Apart from this common pattern, there were marked differences in both the incidence and the types of financial consequences experienced by carers in two-adult households and those in larger households which they shared with a spouse or unmarried sibling as well as the disabled person. However, it was not household size itself which was the important factor, but the relationship between household size and total household income. Unmarried, widowed or divorced carers who were living along with the disabled person had very low incomes on the whole, mainly from social security benefits. When the disability benefits (attendance and mobility allowances) received by the elderly person were taken into account, the incomes of the latter could well be higher than those of their carers. On the other hand, carers living in three-adult households were more likely to be in full- or part-time paid work themselves, and also had access to at least some of the income and other resources of an earning spouse or sibling. This access to at least one income from full-time employment (and often additional earnings from part-time paid work as well) meant that the resources of carers in three-adult households were substantially greater than those of the disabled or elderly person, even when the latter's extra disability benefits were taken into account. These differences in the *relative* income levels of carers and disabled people largely determined both the extent and the nature of the overall financial impact of caring.

Three-adult households

In households which carers shared with a spouse or unmarried sibling as well as the disabled person, the disabled person and the carer (plus spouse or sibling) had very different levels of income. The disabled person relied mainly on income from social security benefits, sometimes supplemented by attendance and mobility allowances, low levels of occupational pensions and savings. The other financial unit(s) in the household – the carers, their partners or their siblings – had considerably higher incomes from at least one full-time wage. Indeed, as we have seen, seven of these 16 households had incomes from one full-time and one part-time wage; and three had incomes from two full-time wages, where both the carer and her/his spouse were in full-time paid work.

These differences in the sources and therefore the levels of income between the two income units within each care-giving household meant that there were also substantial differences in the standards of living which each could normally afford. The imbalance was further accentuated by the fact that the person with the lower income – the disabled or elderly person – was usually living in the household of the person(s) with the much higher income – the carer and her/his partner or sibling.

Together, these factors meant that the income and living standards of the carer and her/his partner or sibling tended to determine the living standards of the whole household. Although much of the disabled person's income was usually available to the carer for collective household expenditure, this was not usually enough to constitute an equal contribution to the standard of living already enjoyed by the carers and their partners or siblings. In the first instance, therefore, carers in three-adult households tended to subsidise the disabled person, by enabling her/him to enjoy a standard of living which was higher than could be afforded by her/his own income alone. Thus some carers considered that their disabled relative's financial contribution did not cover even the basic costs of an additional household member because it was insufficient to pay for an equal share of the commodities and level of comfort enjoyed by the household as a whole:

> I don't know how they manage on their pension, not and eat as well as we eat.
> (*Ms Johnson, married woman caring for her mother*)

> No, she couldn't cope on her own income, not with what she needs. The heating alone would swallow most of that.
> (*Ms Greenwood, single woman who lived with her disabled elderly mother and an unmarried brother*)

Common housing costs and other household overheads which carers continued to pay from their own incomes and to which the disabled person made no explicit contribution represented a further hidden contribution from the carer towards the disabled person's standard of living:

> The thing is, he's in our house, living under our roof, which would still be here if he weren't. So in that way we would still pay the same mortgage . . . the same rates, those sort of overheads.
> (*Ms Rivers, married woman caring for her father-in-law*)

On top of these 'higher standard of living' and 'householder' contributions could be added the extra costs of disability and/or care-giving. Whether these also fell on carers depended on the actual levels of extra spending arising from disablement and caring, on whether the attendance and mobility allowances were received by the disabled person and, if so, whether these were contributed towards relevant areas of household expenditure. The attendance allowance was particularly important in helping to meet these extra costs:

> Perhaps in the beginning we subsidised my mother, because what she got didn't cover what she needed, when she was only on her pension.
> (*Ms Lord, married woman caring for her mother*)

> There was a time when we were subsidising him, but not now, after . . . we learnt that he would possibly be eligible for attendance allowance, which we didn't know about . . . In 1981 I was getting £15 a week from him so in those days we were obviously subsidising him.
> (*Ms Rivers, married woman caring for her father-in-law*)

However, even with the attendance allowance, some carers considered that the income contributed by their disabled relative still to meet their disability and care-related costs. For example, Ms Franks had all of her mother's retirement pension and higher rate attendance allowance. However, from this she had to meet an additional £300 a year on fuel bills, extra on food, clothing, bedding, cleaning items and laundry, £15 a week for a 'sitter' at home, the cost of transport and meals at the day centre, transport to collect incontinence supplies and recent extra expenditure of £75 to replace dentures and spectacles which her mother had lost:

> If we said that she had to make a contribution towards the food and towards the washing and towards the clothes and towards the petrol – if we had very carefully been dividing things up, then I don't suppose it would have been enough.

Taking these three factors into account, in all of the 16 households there was a regular subsidy from the carer to the disabled person, either through the provision of a higher standard of living than could be purchased by the disabled person's income alone or in the form of cost-free accommodation, or both. In half of them the carer was also meeting at least some additional disability and/or care-related costs which were not covered by the disabled person's contribution to the housekeeping. Despite the relatively hidden nature of these financial subsidies, most carers were fully aware of them. In particular, they saw the sharing of their own material quality of life as an integral consequence of giving care in the same household:

> I've never actually sat down and costed it. It's just Mum and I said I would take her.
> (Ms Grey, married woman, whose mother had dementia)

Two-adult households

It was much harder to detect a single clear pattern amongst the carers in two-adult households. Here, the incidence and the types of financial effects of care-giving varied according to sometimes quite small differences in the relative incomes of carers and disabled people and according to the levels of extra costs which caring for a severely disabled person entailed. Three different patterns could be detected.

In the first group, the carer's disposable income was higher than that of the disabled person, because the carer had earnings from employment, because the disabled person received no additional disability benefits such as attendance allowance, or because the disability benefits which were received did not cover very high levels of extra expenses. Here the carer clearly contributed from her/his own resources towards the extra disability and care-related expenses, and sometimes towards some of the disabled person's daily living costs as well. For example, Ms Bryan estimated that caring for her mother involved extra expenditure of £400 a year on heating, extra spending on food (she had no time to 'shop around'), £50 a year on extra laundry and extra on telephone bills. Her mother's income of retirement pension and higher rate attendance allowance was all added to the weekly household kitty or saved towards household bills. Nevertheless, Ms Bryan still had to meet some of these extra costs, as well as their joint housing costs, out of her own income which was derived solely from ICA and savings. In addition Ms Bryan had cut back considerably on her own personal spending – buying new clothes, going out or having holidays – in order to meet her mother's extra needs.

In the second group of two-adult households there appeared, overall, to be very little additional expenditure which fell on carers which was not compensated for by transfers of resources from the disabled person. These households were of two types. Some contained less severely disabled people who incurred few extra disability costs and who also received no additional disability benefits. Both the income levels and consumption patterns of the carers and the disabled people in these households were therefore broadly similar, albeit both very low. Both carers and disabled people were primarily dependent on social security benefits and did not have the additional contribution of the attendance allowance because of the less severe levels of disability involved.

In the second type of 'no extra costs' household, this net effect was achieved only by means of some more complex resource transfers. In these households the carers' incomes and other resources were markedly lower than those of the disabled person, who usually received higher rate attendance allowance and sometimes mobility allowance as well. Moreover, out of these lower incomes carers also helped to carry some of the extra expenses of disabled living. In return, however, some of the disabled person's income or other resources were made available towards the carer's own daily living costs. For example, Ms Peel shared all the household expenditure equally with her friend Jenny. That expenditure included additional fuel costs for heating and laundry, extra bedding, cleaning items and toiletries and higher telephone bills, all because of Jenny's disability. On the face of it, it seemed that Ms Peel's equal contribution to their joint expenditure was in effect subsidising Jenny's higher levels of consumption. However, Jenny gave Ms Peel some of her attendance allowance in return for the care she gave, and also tended to pay for all their social outings and 'treats' out of her considerably higher income (invalidity benefit, higher rate attendance allowance and mobility allowance, compared with Ms Peel's short term rate supplementary benefit).

These carers may not, on balance, have been worse off financially than they would have been had they and the cared-for person adopted more independent systems of financial management. They were, however, worse off in a less tangible sense in that their own financial independence and autonomy had to some extent been eroded, and their standard of living now depended in part on the resources available from the person for whom they were caring.

The financial dependency of the carer was even more marked among the third group of two-adult households. Here, although both the carer and disabled person were again primarily dependent on social security benefits, the person receiving care had some additional financial resources – occupational pensions, higher rate attendance and mobility allowances or savings – which placed them in a relatively advantaged position. Thus when incomes and other household resources were pooled, the higher income of the cared-for person effectively helped to subsidise the carer and maintain her/his standard of living, albeit at a very low level. For example, Ms Harris received just the long-term rate of supplementary benefit. She pooled this with her mother's income of retirement pension, higher rate attendance allowance and the interest from some savings. Although her mother's disablement had doubled their fuel bills to over £600 a year and also created extra expenditure on cleaning items and toiletries, the contribution of her mother's higher income towards their joint household commitments more than covered these extra levels of consumption. Ms Harris' mother also contributed more towards their other joint household commitments than she did. Furthermore, Ms Harris had drawn on her mother's savings for items which were not related to either disability or caring:

> Me mother's kept me in food, she's looked after me dogs, she's paid the vet's bills . . . at 47 years of age I can't see why I should have to live off me mother, because if I have to live off me mother to that extent, what happens when she dies? Who do I live off then?

Anxiety about their longer term financial insecurity was voiced by other carers in this position:

> As an independent person, I'm not well off, I'm getting £23 [ICA] a week and that's it. I'd be a lot better off if I were working, but me mum supports me . . . The only thing that worries me is that if she went into care, it'd leave me high and dry. It gives me a bit of a vulnerable feeling . . . You're taken out of employment, you get

ICA, you're well looked after – in the shadow of me mum. But if anything happens to her, then what happens?
(*Mr Parks, single man who had given up work to look after his mother who had multiple sclerosis*)

For this third group of carers, the cost of caring was impoverishment and a return to a degree of financial dependency on a parent which had been characteristic of their younger, pre-adult status. This renewed financial dependency in their own thirties, forties and fifties was not only far more demeaning than the financial dependency of childhood, but was also considerably more precarious. For these carers current poverty was compounded by considerable longer-term financial insecurity.

Longer term costs and resource transfers

The impact of differences in household size and income levels could also be seen in the longer term patterns of resource transfer between carers and disabled people. There was a marked difference between the two- and three-adult households in the extent to which the savings of disabled people and carers were drawn on and the uses to which they were put.

Use of the disabled person's savings

In the two-adult households, with their very much lower income levels (and in particular the low income levels of the carers), the elderly or disabled person's savings were frequently drawn on for items of common household consumption – fuel, telephone and rates bills and 'one-off' expenditure on repairs or redecoration. They were therefore in part benefiting the carer – a further indication of the way in which the carers in two-adult households tended to be dependent on the resources of the disabled person to maintain their own living standards while giving care.

In contrast, carers living in the higher income three-adult households had far less need to draw on the disabled person's savings to supplement their household income or subsidise items of common household consumption. In some cases these savings were not touched at all; in others they were earmarked specifically for the future purchase of respite or residential care or were used only by the disabled person to buy items for her personal use. They therefore tended not to contribute directly to the living standards of carers in the way that they did in the two-adult households.

Use of the carers' savings

Equally contrasting patterns could be discerned in the use of the carers' savings; in effect, the financial resources which carers transferred to or shared with their disabled relatives over an extended time-scale. Here the contrasts reflected not only differences in household income levels, but also the fact that most of the three-adult households (but very few of the two-adult households) had incurred additional costs in the formation of new joint households in order to provide care.

Carers in the three-adult households tended to experience two types of capital costs: those arising from joint household formation – from having an additional person, albeit sometimes with very specialised needs, join their household; and those arising from their new care-giving role. Almost all of the 16 three-adult households had incurred at least one of these and at least five households had taken out second mortgages or loans to cope with this. In addition, purchases of consumer durables to ease the work of care-giving had all been made from the resources of carers and their partners or siblings.

The two-adult households, in contrast, had generally not incurred additional costs arising from joint household formation, although additional needs did still arise because of disability or to ease the work of care-giving. However, it was noticeable that, because of their lower incomes, these carers were much less likely to bear the costs of these alone. Major adaptations and specialised equipment had almost always come from statutory sources, while other equipment and consumer durables had either been bought jointly with the disabled person, or secondhand from friends who could be repaid gradually as and when money was available. To the extent that part of the money to purchase these items came from the disabled person's own resources, they represented a further enhancement of the living standards of the carer by the disabled or elderly person – but, again, at the expense of her/his own financial independence and autonomy.

Deferred spending and costs

Lastly, there was a greater incidence of deferred spending in the three-adult households than in those which contained only the carer and the disabled person. In at least half of these larger households, carers identified items which they were waiting to repair or replace, either because they were saving up to do so, or because they were waiting until the disabled person was no longer living with them. In contrast, there was no such anticipation of future spending among the two-adult household carers, simply because most of these carers could not envisage being able to afford it. Indeed some of these two-adult households were experiencing even longer term disadvantage by drawing regularly on their savings to maintain their current income. In doing so they were aware that they were contributing to their own long-term impoverishment – particularly in their own eventual old age. This steady depletion of resources was in contrast to the much less regular use of their savings by the carers in the three-adult households – savings which, in any case, they and/or their partners stood a greater chance of replenishing in the longer term because of their continuing higher incomes from paid employment.

Summary 'outcome' measures

Finally a number of indicators were drawn together to reflect the *cumulative* financial impact of care-giving.

Altogether, one or more adverse financial consequences of care-giving were apparent in three-quarters (21) of the 29 households. Three carers reported having to draw on the disabled person's savings and five on their own savings, more than they would otherwise have done. One household was buying more on credit, two delayed paying bills, two carers had cashed insurance policies, nine had cut back on other regular patterns of saving, three had had to borrow money, six had cut down or given up specific items of consumption because money was short and eight carers said that they now worried about money more than they used to.

Only eight carers reported none of these changes, but it was difficult to identify any common characteristics among them. However, among the 21 carers who did report adverse effects, some small differences between the two- and three-adult households were discernible. The carers in the two-adult households reported, on average, twice as many adverse effects as those in three-adult households. Carers in two-adult households were also more likely than those in three-adult households to report having to draw more on their savings or give up or cut back on some item of expenditure since beginning to provide care. These differences are wholly consistent with all the other evidence from this study about the greater degree of impoverishment experienced by carers living alone with the disabled or elderly person. Nevertheless it was clear that the carers in the higher income three-person households were also not immune from at least some effects on their resources and living standards, though this was apparently somewhat less severe.

Developing financial support for informal carers: policies for the future

Despite the central role of informal carers to the success of 'community care', relatively little attention has been given in published policy documents to the question of how family and other carers are to be supported financially.

This study has shown that labour market and employment factors can have a substantial impact on carers' immediate and longer-term financial well-being. However in this policy arena too, informal carers are also apparently being largely overlooked. Yet an issue of increasing concern now is the projected shortfall in labour supply which threatens to increase still further the pressure on women, in particular, to combine paid employment with domestic and caring tasks.

Other important social and economic changes contribute to the overall context within which the implications of this study must be considered. For example, projected changes in mortality rates and marriage patterns have led to forecasts of an increase in the numbers of men who will marry later in life or remain unmarried, thereby becoming heavily involved in the care of elderly parents while remaining at home (Family Policy Studies Centre, 1988, p. 4). Consideration of the financial circumstances of informal carers must also take into account current attitudes towards public expenditure and changes in the role of state welfare provision. These include a growing reliance on private and occupational welfare rather than statutory social security provision during periods when income from earnings is not obtainable, and a reduction in the role of local authorities as direct service providers.

Employment and earnings

Giving help and support to a severely disabled or frail elderly person almost invariably had an adverse effect of some kind on carers' labour market participation. Employment choices and opportunities were extremely restricted (if they existed at all). It was very unusual to have begun or resumed paid employment since starting to care, and most carers who were currently in paid work were simply managing to retain jobs which they had previously held. Around half of them now had reduced earnings, or disposable incomes which were lowered by the purchase of substitute care.

Incomes had also been lost by carers who had given up paid employment altogether because of the disabled person's care needs. Most of them had already lost earnings before finishing work altogether. Around half of the remaining quarter of the sample, who had not been in paid employment at the time they began to provide a great deal of care, were currently unable to re-enter the labour market and knew that this extended period out of work was likely to have an adverse effect on their future employment prospects.

A number of factors apparently helped to facilitate the combination of paid work and care-giving. These included reliable substitute care (and a high enough income to purchase this privately if necessary), a degree of flexibility or autonomy over working arrangements, sympathetic employers, the availability of extended family members to 'keep an eye' on the disabled person and the proximity of work and home.

Combining paid employment with care-giving was very important for a number of reasons. First, paid employment conferred a status and identity outside the home and guaranteed a range of social contacts in an otherwise restricted and isolated life. Secondly, income from paid work was a major source of personal financial resources. (Because of the restricted coverage of the benefit, this remains true even after the 1986 extension of ICA to married women.) Thirdly, because of the low level of ICA, the income which carers could obtain from employment, even on a part-time basis, was almost invariably higher than that which would have been derived from benefit receipt. Fourthly, carers' employment and earnings must be put within the context of total household income. Given the consistently low incomes of the disabled and elderly people receiving care, having one or more wage earners in the household made a crucial difference to the household's total income and, therefore, to its capacity to absorb the extra costs of caring for a disabled or frail elderly person without undue impoverishment. Finally, maintaining paid employment while care-giving had longer-term consequences. Carers who had withdrawn from or been unable to re-enter the labour market anticipated considerable difficulty in returning once the period of caring was over. These difficulties were expected to increase as the period of time out of work lengthened, and were viewed with particular anxiety by carers in their late 40s and 50s. Moreover, carers in households which had no earnings coming in were more likely to be drawing regularly on their own or the disabled person's savings to meet current living expenses. The disadvantage which they anticipated after a lengthy period out of the labour market meant that the chances of being able to replenish these depleted resources before their own retirement were not high.

All these factors highlight the importance of enabling carers to retain – or acquire – paid employment while care-giving, wherever this is desirable and feasible. More widely available day centre or day care provision, for example, would undoubtedly be important here. Such provision should be extensive and flexible enough for carers who work full-time and those who do at least day-time shift work and should also be served by reliable transport facilities – a potential source of further extra expenditure for carers. Where day care facilities away from home are inappropriate, domiciliary-based substitute care arrangements may be necessary. The evidence from this study suggests that such provision may not need to be as specialised and task-focused as that currently provided by conventional home help and community nursing services.

For carers in employment who do not have access to suitable publicly provided day care services and who therefore have to purchase substitute care privately, recognition of these expenses needs to be made. This might be in the form of an additional cash allowance, available to all carers regardless of their employment status or earnings or in the form of tax relief or employer-provided vouchers – the kinds of measures which are currently under discussion in the context of child care provision for mothers in employment (Berry-Lound, 1990).

In addition, contemporary discussions about the organisation and management of paid work could also be of considerable advantage to those with heavy responsibilities for the care of disabled and elderly relatives. Some of these measures, currently being considered in the context of the labour market supply problems of the 1990s, include flexi-time, part-time work, job sharing, and time off work for 'career breaks' or domestic responsibilities (Opportunities for Women, 1990).

However, the evidence from this study of carers should alert us to the scope of some of these proposed measures and the danger that, if adopted, they may be of little or no benefit to those caring for disabled or elderly relatives. Many of these new measures are, typically, to enable women with considerable training or work experience to maintain contact with the labour market during a finite period of childbearing. Such schemes often make no provision for replacing income which is lost during an extended period away from work, and may not be available to male employees. Carers will only stand to benefit from the changes which are being heralded to meet the demands of the labour market over the coming decade if those changes are sufficiently broadly conceived. For example, from the evidence of this small study it seems more appropriate to enable carers to combine paid employment and care-giving, in whatever proportions they feel are practicable, rather than providing for fixed-period breaks from work (even with guarantees of re-employment on return). It would allow carers to avoid the impoverishment and to financial dependency associated with a total loss of earnings and maintain contact with state and occupational pension schemes. This suggests creating greater opportunities for flexi-time, job sharing and part-time working; developing contracts which specify annual rather than daily or weekly hours; and introducing entitlement to a specified number of days of 'compassionate' leave or to care for sick dependants in any one year without loss of pay (Glendinning, 1992).

It does not seem very likely that employers will also begin to take responsibility for substitute care arrangements, in the way they are currently beginning to do through the provision of 'workplace nurseries' and company nannies. Some statutory financial or service provision for employed carers' substitute care needs is therefore an essential complement to any workplace-based changes.

The adequacy and coherence of income maintenance provision

It was clear from this study that social security provision for carers is still far from adequate. The developments in social security which have taken place since the study was carried out, while undoubtedly welcome, do not fundamentally alter this broad conclusion (Glendinning, 1990).

These inadequacies are particularly marked in the case of carers who are unable to retain or resume paid employment. Despite the increase in the take-up of ICA since its extension to married women, coverage of the benefit is still very restricted. It is for example not available to carers who have more than very low incomes from paid work, despite the fact that these may have been substantially reduced by care-giving. Nor can ICA be claimed to offset the substantial substitute care costs experienced by some full-time employed carers.

ICA is also very low. Moreover, because it is taken fully into account in assessments for means-tested benefits and is subject to 'overlapping benefit' restrictions, it offers little advantage to carers in claimant households or who are themselves claiming other benefits. Nevertheless for non-employed carers with savings above the capital limit for means-tested benefits, ICA – at less than four-fifths (79 per cent in 1991/2) of the income support adult personal allowance – may be their only source of income.

Other problems are created by the linking of entitlement to ICA with the disabled person's receipt of attendance allowance. Non-receipt of the latter benefit (for whatever reason) removes the carer's entitlement to an income of her/his own. Moreover, Home Responsibilities Protection of the state retirement pension, entitlement to means-tested income support without having to register for work and entitlement to the new income support 'carer' premium are all ultimately dependent upon the same condition. Thus carers may find both their current income and their future pension entitlements jeopardised because of the disabled person's failure to claim or qualify for attendance allowance. The evidence from this small study suggests that such take-up problems may not be uncommon. Where there is friction or disagreement between carers and disabled people, these problems of interacting benefit entitlements are likely to be compounded.

There is no social security provision at all for carers past statutory retirement age, even if they have continued working past that age and then had to stop because of care-giving. With discussions of increasing flexibility around the age of retirement, such a rigid age limit may need reassessment. The study also revealed considerable financial insecurity for carers if the disabled person dies or enters residential care, particularly if the carer is to some extent financially dependent upon the person being cared for. The extension in 1991 of the income support carer premium for eight weeks after care-giving ceases may still be too short to compensate for the disadvantage experienced by some carers after a prolonged period out of the labour market. ICA claimants and other carers whose incomes have been substantially reduced by care-giving, but who do not receive income support, still do not have even this limited protection after they cease providing care (see McLaughlin, 1991 for a detailed discussion of ICA).

It is also important to note that there is no private or occupational income maintenance provision for informal carers. On the contrary, breaks in employment or periods of reduced earnings because of care-giving will have an adverse effect on eventual retirement pension levels. Moreover there is no occupational equivalent for carers to maternity pay or sick pay, which might guarantee some continued income during periods of caring; and, as mentioned above, 'career break' schemes which might be used for periods of informal care-giving are not accompanied by occupationally derived income.

There are a number of priorities, then, in considering the development of social security policies for carers. First, because of the capital cut-off for means-tested income support and housing benefit, some carers have to depend entirely on invalid care allowance as their sole source of income. In these circumstances the present level of ICA is unacceptably low and needs to be raised, preferably to the level of long-term benefits such as invalidity or old age pensions, as recommended recently by the House of Commons Social Services Committee (House of Commons, 1990a). Carers with substantial levels of savings might thereby avoid eating into these to the extent that they eventually become dependent on means-tested income support. It would also direct resources to two of the main groups of working age carers who currently receive very little direct advantage from ICA – those who are affected by overlapping personal benefit regulations, and those whose claimant partners lose a 'dependant's' addition to their own benefit when the carer claims ICA. A much higher level of ICA would offer such carers a higher level of income than would be available from these other benefit entitlements.

It is, nevertheless, important to recognise that this measure would not direct any additional financial resources to carers who are currently over pension age, whether they begin giving care before or after that age. Whether and how this might be done is an issue which must remain of some importance.

Secondly, recognition needs to be given to the loss of disposable income (whether through reduced earnings or high substitute care costs) experienced by carers in paid work. This might be achieved by a further increase in the earnings limit on ICA, with a gradual tapered withdrawal of the benefit above that limit, either in conjunction with, or as an alternative to, tax relief on substitute care costs as mentioned above. These measures would also help to reduce disincentives to seeking employment or increasing earnings while caring which might be created by the anticipated loss of benefit – a kind of carers' 'poverty trap'. Thirdly, ICA should automatically attract full protection of all national insurance benefit entitlements.

Finally, carers' entitlements to a basic income of their own should not be contingent upon the benefits received by the person being cared for. This linkage compromises the principle set out in the 1974 White

Paper which first proposed the introduction of ICA (DHSS, 1974), that carers should have an entitlement to an *independent* income of their own.

This principle is also important for other reasons. The study showed that, in the vast majority of cases, it was the carer who was responsible for all the day-to-day household budgeting, including the purchase of extra commodities or services which were needed because of disability, or to ease the work of care-giving. This issue is considerably more problematic here than it is in relation to the care of children, disabled or otherwise, where benefits are paid to parents who are then expected to spend them on the child's behalf. Here, benefits for both basic income maintenance and the extra costs of disability are paid to the elderly person, who may then transfer some or all of them at her/his discretion to the person who is responsible for the routine financial management of the household in which they live. In practice, so far as the evidence from this research is con-cerned, this transfer of resources from one person to another within the same household was relatively unproblematic. Indeed in many instances the type and degree of disability of the cared-for person meant that s/he had effectively relinquished all control over her/his own financial affairs. In other circumstances however, conflicts may be more common, with some elderly people being unwilling to transfer some or all of their income to the person responsible for the household's financial management and expenditure. While it is not possible to legislate against such situations, there may be arguments for ensuring that carers are protected, through access to an indepen-dent income of their own, from any gross financial hardship which would otherwise ensue.

The extra expenses of disability and care-giving

The study identified a range of extra expenditure incurred by carers which was not covered by the resources of the disabled or elderly person. The incidence of extra costs depended substantially on the income level of the household and on the circumstances in which care-giving began, as well as on the type and degree of disability of the disabled person. In households which had been formed specifi-cally for the purposes of giving care (typically, when an elderly person moved into the household of a son or daughter), some additional 'lump sum' outlays were common. These tended to be for items needed to accommodate an additional person in comfort – building an additional room, installing extra heating, enlarging the bathroom, buying new beds, chairs, tables and extra television sets.

Both these newly formed households and those where the carer and disabled person had lived together long before the onset of care-giving also incurred extra expenditure to ease the work of caring. Many carers had bought washing machines and tumble driers, some had purchased commodes, telephones, microwaves, freezers and larger cars, or had installed more convenient heating appliances, even when their own incomes were low or in the context of substantial other extra expenses.

Such expenditure often occurred early in the giving of care. Other extra spending associated with care-giving – redecoration, replacing damaged floorcoverings, bedding and furniture – was sometimes deferred until the period of care-giving was over. Policies which might help carers recoup some of this additional expenditure must therefore take account of its timing.

Since 1988 the Independent Living Fund (ILF) has been established to assist with the purchase of care, including the cost of special equipment which might help reduce the costs of giving care. In practice, however, relatively few applications are made to the ILF for such equipment. Similarly, the community care grant element of the Social Fund can provide help to income support claimants who might otherwise be at risk of entering residential care. Again, however, it seems that relatively few grants are made towards the types of expenditure incurred by some carers in providing suitable furnishings, equipment and accommodation when setting up new, joint households (DSS, 1991).

Carers also experienced more regular spending associated with care-giving, apart from the cost of substitute care. This included extra transport and telephone costs, hospital visiting costs, and the purchase of extra books, records and videos for home entertainment (some of which was balanced by reduced spending on outings and holidays).

Most carers also had extra expenditure caused by the disability of the person being given care, the most common of which was extra heating and spending associated with incontinence – laundry, toiletries, cleaning items and the replacement of damaged or worn bedding and clothing. Extra spending on food and on transport for disabled people with mobility problems were also fairly common.

The analysis of household budgeting and expenditure patterns which was carried out in this study took full account of the resources contributed by the disabled person. Nevertheless, in many instances at least some of these extra disability costs still fell on carers to meet out of their own financial resources. In addition, some carers incurred extra expenditure because they provided their disabled or elderly relatives with a higher standard of living than s/he would have been able to afford from her/his own income alone. In the poorer households, hidden 'costs' were experienced by carers, including the foregoing of items of consumption in order to meet the disability costs of the disabled person, and the psychological 'costs' of their own financial dependency.

In a few instances these disability costs fell on carers because the disabled person was not claiming benefits for which s/he would have been eligible or because s/he did not contribute enough of her income towards the items and services which were purchased on her behalf. In the majority of cases, carers carried some of the extra costs of disability simply because the incomes of their disabled and elderly relatives were too low to meet their needs. Furthermore they were always too low to provide the disabled person with the same standard of living as that enjoyed by an earning carer.

These conclusions have implications for debates about 'relative' definitions of poverty and about the importance of looking at individual as well as household incomes and consumption patterns in measuring poverty. The findings also call into question the adequacy of disabled people's incomes, particularly when disability occurs in old age, and about the effectiveness of current social security provision which is intended to meet the extra costs of disability. Significantly, the recent review of benefits for disabled people includes no new measures to assist disabled people over pension age (DSS, 1990a), while evidence on the adequacy of existing extra costs disability benefits remains highly controversial (DIG, 1988, 1990; House of Commons, 1990b). The important point to be drawn from this research is that these issues have substantial implications for carers' financial circumstances too.

It is important to note in this concluding discussion that no account has been taken of the value of carers' time – a huge resource which has not been costed in this study. Nor has any attempt been made to assess whether care-giving has social or psychological 'costs' which might be assigned a notional financial value. It is a matter for debate as to whether and how any such 'costs' might be reduced. It is also open for discussion as to whether, and to what extent, carers should be expected to meet the outstanding financial costs of care-giving from their own resources. However, in view of the centrality of informal carers to the success and effectiveness of 'community care', there are strong arguments for providing additional help towards all these various 'costs'. One way to do this might be to introduce a carer's costs allowance, non-means-tested, payable regardless of age, sex and marital status and disregarded for other means-tested benefits. This would help to meet some of the outstanding capital and recurrent costs associated with care-giving. It would also help to direct financial assistance towards carers over retirement age who currently receive no extra financial support at all.

Many of the financial costs currently borne by carers, as well as the psychological and social stresses they experience, would also be vastly reduced by increased inputs of services, including day and substitute care services. Adequate incontinence services can make an enormous impact on both the additional costs borne by carers and the physical work involved. Laundry services and the wider availability of help with housing alterations, heating installations and more specialised equipment would have similar effects. Service intervention can also offer opportunities for maximising the independence of both carers and disabled people, whether they are living together as in this study, or not (Beardshaw, 1988; Fiedler, 1988).

Ultimately, the extent to which the financial consequences of 'community care' fall on individual carers, with little or no recompense, rests on political decisions about the allocation of economic resources. However, the social, demographic and policy changes which form the framework of this study provide a context of imperatives which are likely to become increasingly urgent.

Bibliography

BALDWIN, S. (1985) *The Costs of Caring*. London: Routledge and Kegan Paul.

BEARDSHAW, V. (1988) *Last on the List: Community Services for People with Physical Disabilities*. London: Kings Fund Institute.

BERRY-LOUND, D. (1990) *Work and the Family*. London: Institute of Personnel Management.

BRADSHAW, J. (1980) *The Family Fund: An Initiative in Social Policy*. London: Routledge and Kegan Paul.

BRANNEN, J. and WILSON, G. (eds) (1987) *Give and Take in Families: Studies in Resource Distribution*. London: Allen and Unwin.

BRENTON, M. (1985) *The Voluntary Sector in British Social Services*. London: Longman.

BUCKLE, J. (1984) *Mental Handicap Costs More*. London: Disablement Income Group.

CHALLIS, D. and DAVIES, B. (1980) 'A New Approach to Community Care for the Elderly.' *British Journal of Social Work*, 10, i, pp. 1–18.

CHALLIS, D., LUCKETT, R. and CHESSUM, R. (1983) 'A New Life at Home.' *Community Care*, 455, 24 March.

DEPARTMENT OF HEALTH AND SOCIAL SECURITY (1974) *Social Security Provision for Chronically Sick and Disabled People*, HC276. London: HMSO.

DEPARTMENT OF HEALTH AND SOCIAL SECURITY (1981) *Growing Older: White Paper on Services for Elderly People*, Cmnd. 8173. London: HMSO.

DEPARTMENT OF HEALTH AND SOCIAL SECURITY (1985) *Reform of Social Security: Programme for Action*, Cmnd. 9691. London: HMSO.

DH/DSS/WELSH OFFICE/SCOTTISH HHD (1989) *Caring for People: Community Care in the Next Decade and Beyond*, Cm. 849. London: HMSO.

DEPARTMENT OF SOCIAL SECURITY (1990a) *The Way Ahead: Benefits for Disabled People*, Cm. 917. London: HMSO.

DEPARTMENT OF SOCIAL SECURITY (1990b) *Disability, Household Income and Expenditure*, Research Report No. 2. London: HMSO.

DEPARTMENT OF SOCIAL SECURITY (1991) *Annual Report by the Secretary of State for Social Security on the Social Fund 1990–1*, Cm. 1580. London: HMSO.

DIG (1988) *Not the OPCS Survey: Being Disabled Costs More Than They Said.* London: Disablement Income Group.

DIG (1990) *Short Changed by Disability*. London: Disablement Income Group.

FAMILY POLICY STUDIES CENTRE (1988) *Family Policy Bulletin*, 5, Summer. London: FPSC.

FAMILY POLICY STUDIES CENTRE (1989) *Family Policy Bulletin*, 6, Winter. London: FPSC.

FIEDLER, B. (1988) *Living Options Lottery*. London: Prince of Wales' Advisory Group on Disability.

FINCH, J. and GROVES, D. (1980) 'Community Care and the Family: A Case for Equal Opportunities?' *Journal of Social Policy*, 9, 4, pp. 487–511.

FINCH, J. and GROVES, D. (eds) (1983) *A Labour of Love: Women, Work and Caring*. London: Routledge and Kegan Paul.

GLENDINNING, C. (1983) *Unshared Care: Families with Disabled Children*. London: Routledge and Kegan Paul.

GLENDINNING, C. (1990) 'Dependency and Interdependency: The Incomes of Informal Carers and the Impact of Social Security.' *Journal of Social Policy*, 19, 4, pp. 469–97.

GLENDINNING, C. (1992) 'Employment and Community Care: Policies for the 1990s.' *Work, Employment and Society*, 6, 1.

GLENDINNING, C. and MILLAR, J. (eds) (1987) *Women and Poverty in Britain*. Brighton: Wheatsheaf Books.

GLENNESTER, H. (1985) *Paying for Welfare*. Oxford: Basil Blackwell.

GRAHAM, H. (1983), 'Caring: A Labour of Love.' In FINCH, J. and GROVES, D. (eds), *A Labour of Love: Women, Work and Caring*. London: Routledge and Kegan Paul.

GRAHAM, H. (1987), 'Women's Poverty and Caring.' In GLENDIN-NING, C. and MILLAR, J. (eds) *Women and Poverty in Britain.* Brighton: Wheatsheaf Books.

GREEN, H. (1988) *Informal Carers.* General Household Survey, 1985. London: HMSO.

GRIFFITHS, R. (1988) *Community Care: Agenda for Action.* London: HMSO.

HENWOOD, M. (1990) *Community Care and Elderly People.* London: Family Policy Studies Centre.

HIRST, M. (1985) 'Young Adults with Disabilities: Health, Employment and Financial Costs for Family Carers.' *Child: Care, Health and Development,* 11, 5, pp. 291–307.

HORTON, C. and BERTHOUD, R. (1990) *The Attendance Allowance and the Costs of Caring.* London: Policy Studies Institute.

HOUSE OF COMMONS (1990a) *Community Care: Carers.* Social Services Committee Fifth Report 1989–90. London: HMSO.

HOUSE OF COMMONS (1990b) *Community Care: Social Security for Disabled People,* Social Services Committee Ninth Report, HC646. London: HMSO.

JOSHI, H. (1987) 'The Cost of Caring.' In GLENDINNING, C. and MILLAR, J. (eds) *Women and Poverty in Britain.* Brighton: Wheatsheaf Books.

LAND, H. and ROSE, H. (1985) 'Compulsory Altruism for all or an Altruistic Society for Some?' In BEAN, P., FERRIS, J. and WHYNES, D. (eds) *In Defence of Welfare.* London: Tavistock.

LEVIN, E., SINCLAIR, I. and GORBACH, P. (1989) *Families, Services and Confusion in Old Age.* Aldershot: Avebury.

LEWIS, J. and MEREDITH, B. (1988) *Daughters Who Care: Daughters Caring for Mothers at Home.* London: Routledge.

LONSDALE, S. (1987) 'Patterns of Paid Work.' In GLENDINNING, C. and MILLAR, J. (eds) *Women and Poverty in Britain.* Brighton: Wheatsheaf Books.

MARTIN, J. and ROBERTS, C. (1984) *Women and Employment: A Lifetime Perspective.* London: HMSO.

MARTIN, J. and WHITE, A. (1988) *The Financial Circumstances of Disabled Adults Living in Private Households.* London: HMSO.

McLAUGHLIN, E. (1991) *Social Security and Community Care: The Case of the Invalid Care Allowance.* London: HMSO.

NISSEL, M. and BONNERJEA, L. (1982) *Family Care of the Handicapped Elderly – Who Pays?* London: Policy Studies Institute.

OPPORTUNITIES FOR WOMEN (1990) *Care to Work*, National Carers Survey, Vol. 1, Survey Report. London: OFW.

PAHL, J. (1988) 'Earning, Sharing, Spending.' In WALKER, R. and PARKER, G. (eds) *Money Matters: Income, Wealth and Financial Welfare.* London: Sage.

PAHL, J. (1989) *Money and Marriage.* Basingstoke: Macmillan.

PARKER, G. (forthcoming) *With this Body: Caring, Disability and Marriage.* Buckingham: Open University Press.

PARKER, G. (1990) *With Due Care and Attention:* a review of research on informal care (2nd Edition) London: Family Policy Studies Centre.

QURESHI, H. and WALKER, A. (1989) *The Caring Relationship.* Basingstoke: Macmillan.

RIMMER, L. (1983) 'The Economics of Work and Caring.' In FINCH, J. and GROVES, D. (eds) *A Labour of Love: Women, Work and Caring.* London: Routledge and Kegan Paul.

SMYTH, M. and ROBUS, N. (1989) *The Financial Circumstances of Families with Disabled Children Living in Private Households.* London: HMSO.

SPENCE, A. (1990) 'Labour Force Outlook to 2001.' *Employment Gazette*, April, pp.186–98.

UNGERSON, C. (1987) *Policy is Personal: Sex, Gender and Informal Care.* London: Tavistock.

WALKER, A. (ed) (1982) *Community Care: The Family, the State and Social Policy.* Oxford: Basil Blackwell and Martin Robertson.

WEBB, A. and WISTOW, G. (1987) *Social Work, Social Care and Social Planning.* London: Longman.

WENGER, G.C. (1984) *The Supportive Network.* Hemel Hempstead: Allen and Unwin.

WRIGHT, F. (1986) *Left to Care Alone.* Aldershot: Gower.

WRIGHT, K., CAIRNS, J. and SNELL, M. (1981) *Costing Care.* Sheffield: University of Sheffield/Community Care.

Index

Printed in the United Kingdom for HMSO
Dd295184 2/92 C13 531/2 10170